I WILL ESPOUSE YOU FOREVER

More praise for *I Will Espouse You Forever*:

"This book is a signal moment in the growing realization that divine love and human love of God are central motifs in the Hebrew Bible. Its great contribution is to uncover the ways that temple and Torah are the centers of the intimacy of Israel and its people with God. The Song then provides the important base for rediscovering and claiming that intimacy and love when the temple disappears. Especially important is Lyke's demonstration of why it is that the history of interpretation of the Song is not a secondary matter but the primary way into the text."
— Patrick D. Miller, Professor of Old Testament Theology Emeritus, Princeton Theological Seminary

"Larry Lyke has written a wonderful book about the theology of love in the Hebrew Bible. Making expert use of modern and traditional methods of reading, he examines how God's deep passion for his people is presumed in the prophets and the object of conscious reflection in early interpretation—the Targum to the Song, the Midrash, and Origen's Homily and Commentary. Well written and argued, *I Will Espouse You Forever* is a superb contribution to our understanding of the Song and to the increasingly important biblical theology that takes account of Jewish as well as Christian tradition."
— Richard J. Clifford, S.J., Professor of Old Testament, Weston Jesuit School of Theology, Cambridge, Massachusetts

"Taking his cue from the intertextual readings of the ancient rabbis and church fathers, Lyke demonstrates that these interpreters were attuned to canonical theological and literary tropes that historical criticism overlooks. This innovative and accessible book unlocks one of the most cryptic biblical texts by recovering the ancient assumptions that not only illuminate its traditional interpretation, but explain its canonical status."
— Joel S. Kaminsky, Associate Professor, Department of Religion, Director of the Program in Jewish Studies, Smith College

"In this remarkable book, Lyke shows us how the Song of Songs evolved from a set of human love songs to a theological reflection on the passion God feels for his people, Israel. Though most interpreters have found this radical transformation to be late in origin and artificial in nature, Lyke shows the reader how the religion of the Hebrew Bible itself already pointed in the direction of interpreting the Song of Songs in this way. Indeed, given the type of literary competence that was evolving in ancient Israel, it is hard to see how the poems could be read in any other way."
— Gary Anderson, Professor of Hebrew Bible/Old Testament, Department of Theology, Notre Dame University

"In a concise and entirely persuasive manner, Larry Lyke demonstrates *how* the Song of Songs came to be regarded by both Jews and early Christians as the interpretive key for reading the Bible's deepest theological claim: the unfailing love of God for God's people."
— Brooks Schramm, Associate Professor of Biblical Studies, Lutheran Theological Seminary, Gettysburg, Pennsylvania

I Will Espouse You Forever

The Song of Songs

and the Theology of Love

in the Hebrew Bible

LARRY L. LYKE

Abingdon Press
Nashville

I WILL ESPOUSE YOU FOREVER
THE SONG OF SONGS AND THE THEOLOGY OF LOVE IN THE HEBREW BIBLE

Copyright © 2007 by Abingdon Press

This book is printed on acid-free paper.

Library of Congress Cataloging-in-Publication Data

Lyke, Larry L.
I will espouse you forever : the Song of Songs and the theology of love in the Hebrew Bible / Larry L. Lyke.
    p. cm.
Includes bibliographical references and index.
ISBN 978-0-687-64574-9 (pbk : alk. paper)
    1. Bible. O.T. Song of Solomon—Criticism, interpretation, etc. 2. Love—Biblical teaching. 3. Bible.
O.T.—Criticism, interpretation, etc. I. Title.

BS1485.52.L95 2007
223'.906—dc22

2007029457

Hebrew Bible excerpts, unless otherwise noted, are from *The TANAKH: The New JPS Translation According to the Traditional Hebrew Text.* Copyright 1985 by the Jewish Publication Society. Used by permission.

Quotations noted NRSV are from the New Revised Standard Version of the Bible, copyright 1989, Division of Christian Education of the National Council of the Churches of Christ in the United States of America. Used by permission. All rights reserved.

Quotations noted RSV are from the Revised Standard Version of the Bible, copyright 1952 [2nd edition, 1971] by the Division of Christian Education of the National Council of the Churches of Christ in the United States of America. Used by permission. All rights reserved.

Quotations from the Targum, Mishnah, and Song of Songs are the author's translation.

Hebrew Bible quotations noted AT are the author's translation.

Excerpts from *Origen, The Song of Songs, Commentary and Homilies (ACW 25)*, translated and annotated by R.P. Lawson, copyright © 1957 by Rev. Johannes Quasten, STD and Rev. Joseph C. Plumpe, PhD. Used with permission of The Newman Press, an imprint of Paulist Press, Inc., New York/Mahwah, N.J. www.paulistpress.com.

07 08 09 10 11 12 13 14 15 16—10 9 8 7 6 5 4 3 2 1
MANUFACTURED IN THE UNITED STATES OF AMERICA

TO THE MEMORY of my mother, Lucille Ellen Lyke

CONTENTS

ACKNOWLEDGMENTS

T he making of many books is without limit" (Qoh 12:12) is often cited at the beginning of a book as a form of apology for adding yet one more tome to an already long list of treatments on one topic or another. This part of the verse can just as easily be translated, "The making of many books is without end." It is in this variant sense that I understand the verse, given the nearly ten years this work was in the making. As a result, there are a number of people whom I wish to thank whose patience has been remarkable.

First, I must thank John Kutsko Ph.D., Director of Academic and Ministry Leadership Resources at Abingdon Press, who has been unstinting in his support of this project from its inception. In addition to his support, his encouragement and feedback have been invaluable. The manuscript is far better for his guidance, and to him I am deeply indebted. I would also like to thank Sarah Hasenmueller, copy editor at Abingdon, for her keen eye and tireless work in making this a better book.

I am also indebted to the Department of Religion at Trinity College, Hartford. My colleagues there have listened attentively on many occasions to my musings on topics covered in this work. I thank them for their patience and support, even when things did not turn out as we had hoped. In particular, I wish to thank Professor Patricia Byrne C.S.J. for listening to many of the ideas that appear herein and for her continually positive feedback.

Gary Anderson and Jon Levenson agreed to read an early form of the manuscript and I thank them both for their quick and helpful responses. Clearly, I am at fault for any remaining errors in fact, judgment, or interpretation. Professor Levenson, in particular, has been a great help both in the conception of this book and in its coming to fruition. Seldom does one have such a good and erudite ear for one's work.

No book, or idea contained therein, arises in a vacuum. This author is in a continuum with so many who have come before that it is impossible, within the limits of these acknowledgments, to identify them all. Suffice it to say that I am indebted to the great minds who precede me, including those whose efforts created and maintained the fascinating traditions about which I write in this book. I am compelled to cite one of my favorite rabbinic sayings:

> Yose ben Yoezer said:
> Let your house be a gathering place for the sages,
> Sit in the dust at their feet,
> Drink in with thirst their words. (*m. Abot* 1:4)

Quotations from the Hebrew Bible contained herein are from the *Tanakh* (Philadelphia: Jewish Publication Society, 5745/1985). I have indicated when I vary from their version. Translations of the New Testament and Apocryphal literature come from the NRSV unless otherwise specified. Translation of the Targum and midrash to the Song of Songs are my own. Transliteration of Hebrew and Aramaic follows the simplified and general purpose form provided by the *Society of Biblical Literature Handbook of Style* (Peabody: Hendrickson, 1999). This transliteration lacks the precision of the scholarly form but makes the text more accessible to a general audience. Because Hebrew and Aramaic, like the other Semitic languages, are based on a triliteral root system (each word arises from a root comprised of three consonants), I have provided the Hebrew or Aramaic root of important words in parentheses in order that readers may follow the argument more closely. Scholarly convention uses the abbreviations B.C.E. and C.E. for the more well-known forms B.C. and A.D. I render the Tetragrammaton (YHWH, the four-letter name for God) without vowels. Finally, because the Hebrew Bible consistently conceives of God as grammatically masculine and because God is persistently understood as husband in the texts we consider in this work, I have used masculine pronouns in reference to *him*.

INTRODUCTION

I slept but my heart was aroused, the sound of my lover knocking,
Open for me, my dear sister—my perfect dove,
For my head is filled with dew, my locks with the drops of night.
I had removed my robe, should I put it on again?
I had washed my feet, should I soil them?
My love withdrew his hand from the hollow, and my heart sank,
I arose to open for my love, my hand flowing with myrrh,
My fingers pouring with myrrh, upon the handle.
I opened for my love, but my love had turned away,
My very soul went out at his word,
I sought him but did not find him, I called but he did not answer.

Thus reads Song of Songs 5:2-6. It is hard to miss the sexually explicit nature of its references even if they are couched in metaphor. I have a friend and colleague who often jokes, "I have not read the Song of Songs; I am waiting for the movie!" Clearly, should a film adaptation appear, one would find it in the adult section of the local video store. This realization is, perhaps, even more startling considering general biblical teaching on sexuality. Based on texts as far ranging as Lev 18–20 or 1 Cor 7, strictures on human sexuality predominate. Given the biblical tendency to regulate and restrict sexual activity, what should we make of the moving encounters described in the Song of Songs? Why is this text in the Bible?[1] Cheryl Exum, in her commentary on the Song of Songs, puts the question this way, "How did a poem celebrating human love and desire, a text that contains no religious teaching and in which God is not mentioned, come to be included in a collection of sacred writings?" She continues with a response that represents current scholarly consensus: "To this fascinating question the simple answer is: we do not know."[2] The present work attempts to flesh out a reasonable response to the question that has remained unanswered. The short answer is that early in its reception, the Song of Songs came to be associated with the love of God for Israel and for the church. This answer, however, begs another question, namely, *How could anyone read the text above to mean anything other than what it obviously, albeit metaphorically, says?*

In the course of the following study we set out to establish precisely the literary and cultural competence that came to understand the Song of Songs as part of the theology of love in the Hebrew Bible. By *theology of love* we refer to a tradition that, in the earliest Jewish and Christian interpretations, understood the Song of Songs to be about God's deep passion for his people.[3] In their own turns, both Jews and Christians came to cherish the Song of Songs for what they saw as God's eternal declaration of devotion and desire. Early Jewish interpretation understood the Song to address their long affair with God, beginning with the courtship during the exodus and looking forward to an imagined third temple. These historical bookmarks imply the memory of, and future hope for, God's intimate presence. Indeed, the term *theology of love* is coined precisely because it captures this notion. Early Christian interpretation, likewise, presumed that the Song was about the ongoing intimacy of God with his people. For these Christians, however, the Song was about God's love expressed as Christ's love for the church and, simultaneously, the desire of the human soul for God and his Word.

The term *theology of love* finds its locus in early interpretation as a way of understanding those interpreters' assumption that the erotic language in the Song of Songs is used to describe theological reality. Whatever one makes of the imagination required to understand the Song's sensuality in this way, we might ask, *Is there biblical warrant for such understanding?* The purpose of part 1 of this study is to answer this question affirmatively. The forms of the theology of love found in a number of texts in the Hebrew Bible are, indeed, the origin of early interpreters' presumptions. As a means to lay the foundations of our understanding of the theology of love, in chapter 1 we shall first look to the prophetic tradition. In the prophetic idiom, the theology of love presumes that God is married to Israel. For the prophets, the marriage is damaged to the point of breaking because of Israel's apostasy, understood as infidelity to the God of Israel. The first text that explicitly presumes a marriage relationship between God and Israel is Hosea. In turn, Jeremiah, Nahum, and Ezekiel take up the metaphor of marriage and adultery to describe what they view as Israel's apostasy in worshiping other gods. With passionate rhetoric, the prophets that we shall look at below border on the obscene in representing God's vehement rejection of Israel's behavior. We shall consider the ways in which the marriage metaphor seemed to take root in the prophetic idiom and, likewise, consider its evolution. As it turns out, we shall see that a constellation of language and imagery came to be associated with what we shall call the marriage/adultery motif. Most significant for our study are the association of apostasy with adultery and the concomitant presumption of defilement. As we shall see, in later texts like Ezek 23, this defilement is associated, in particular, with the temple. As a result, the temple, subject to the defilement brought on by Israel's "adultery," can be understood as a woman to whom God has the exclusively legitimate claim.

It is the significance of the temple in the evolution of the theology of love that we take up in chapter 2, which is entitled, "The Temple, Women, and Wombs." In this chapter we shall begin with Ezek 24 in which the author associates the temple with a woman. While defilement is not mentioned, it is the loss of Ezekiel's wife that is a foreshadowing of the destruction of the first temple in this text. We pursue the association of the temple as a woman raped in Lamentations, to its fullest articulation in the book of Judith. It is in this final text that we see most clearly what seem to be the assumptions embedded in the temple-as-woman motif. In chapter 9, Judith claims that the temple is on the verge of being penetrated and defiled, as was Dinah in Gen 34. Here, much like in Lamentations, the temple is understood as the inviolable space that only God can enter. Judith 9 reflects much of biblical tradition that understood the temple to be God's residence and the holy of holies, in particular, to be off limits to all but him. We shall discover that Judith represents the fruition of the temple-as-woman motif and, as such, points to the temple as one of the two main pillars that supported the edifice of the theology of love in the late Second Temple period. One of the guarantees of God's presence and beneficence was the very existence of his residence, the temple. That his residence was also associated with his mate makes its loss even more compelling.

That Judith could see the temple as vulnerable to defilement, indeed, as a woman raped, has clear connections to the developments we trace in the prophetic tradition in chapter 1 and leads us to investigate the second pillar of the theology of love in the late Second Temple period. Like the first, the second pillar of the theology of love is formulated in the imagery of women. In chapter 3, entitled "Women, Wells, Wisdom, and Torah," we consider the imagery of wells and their association with women and fertility. At early stages only vague and highly symbolic, this association evolves through the developing biblical corpus until in the late Second Temple period when we see the association of women, wells, Wisdom and, ultimately, Torah. We begin with an analysis of a number of passages in Genesis through Exod 2 in which we see women and wells serve as ciphers for each other. We then trace the emergence in the Wisdom tradition of the association of women, wells, and Wisdom. In the idiom of Prov 5, Wisdom represents a kind of divine feminine principle to which Israel and individual Israelites owe devotion. Our discussion leads to an investigation of Sir 24 in which the author makes explicit his assumption that Wisdom, as a woman and life-sustaining water, is none other than Torah. Of special interest in this text, Sirach describes Wisdom and Torah in language so resonant with the Song of Songs it is difficult to imagine that the two are not related, if only in Sirach's mind. In chapter 24 of Sirach we have all the ingredients that compose the theology of love in the early interpretive tradition.

What is remarkable about these two pillars of the theology of love that rise to support the theological assumptions of the late Second Temple period is that each represents the divine in feminine imagery. While God remains conceived as male, his temple and "mate" is obviously female. In this theological construct, God's very presence among his people is dependent on the maintenance of the purity of the temple, his bride. In the second instance, Wisdom comes to represent a form of divine presence, perhaps less subject to defilement, but held in equally high regard. It is in the intimacy of God's presence in the temple and in Wisdom, understood as Torah, that late Second Temple Jews invested so heavily. Embedded in these two foci of the theology of love was the implicit assertion that God's desire for his people was ongoing and eternal. Of course, such an assertion is unnecessary, absent the anxiety instilled by a long history of disappointment.

Indeed, the evolution of the theology of love can be understood, from its inception, in light of anxiety over God's presence and commitment to the marriage.[4] In particular, the prophetic marriage/adultery motif is, at least in part, a response to impending disaster. Hosea's use of the motif comes on the eve of the Assyrian destruction of the northern kingdom of Samaria in ca. 722 B.C.E. Jeremiah and Ezekiel employ the motif in light of the impending neo-Babylonian invasion or in its immediate wake. It was the crisis that arose from the destruction of the first temple in ca. 587 B.C.E. that provided the initial impetus to invest in the two great conceptions that are our focus in part 1. That Jews were subjugated to foreign powers until the destruction of the second temple exacerbated an already intolerable reality. As a result, on the one hand, Jews invested in the hope that the temple would continue to provide the locus of God's presence and ongoing intimacy. On the other hand, there was a simultaneous investment in the notion that God's presence and intimacy were to be found in the emergent textual tradition that would eventually come to be known as Torah. In the language, metaphor, and imagery of sexual intimacy, the texts we investigate in part 1 of our study consistently depict their authors' theological desire.

To the degree that the destruction of the first temple encouraged investment in the two pillars of the theology of love, the destruction of the second temple in 70 C.E. destroyed one of them. In response to this deep loss, the theology of love had little choice but to double its investment in Torah.[5] To a large degree, the coalescence of the Bible itself is a function of this reallocation. We shall see in the second part of this study the ways in which early Jewish and Christian interpretation insist on the sanctity of Scripture and see in it the guarantee of God's continuing presence. The Song of Songs, in particular, came to be understood as the text of all texts for revealing the eternal passion and desire of God for his people.[6] Indeed, the Song became the focal point of the lens through which early interpreters viewed the theology of love in the Hebrew Bible. It might seem odd, then, that even after the destruction of the second temple, interpreters of both traditions continued to conceive of God's presence in imagery related to the temple as well. We shall see that, while the written traditions gained ascendancy, the temple and traditions associated with it persisted even after its destruction. While the biblical texts that we shall consider in part 1 merely presume the theology of love, the interpretive traditions that are our focus in part 2 set about to articulate it. In so doing, they turn to the rest of what they know as Scripture to elaborate on the history of God's love affair with his people. In this respect, they reveal their remarkable literary competence in their assumption that the Song of Songs is part (and the best example) of the tradition of the theology of love in the Hebrew Bible.

In chapter 4 we turn to the Aramaic translation, known as the Targum, of the Song of Songs to see how early Jewish interpretation understood the Song. The Targum's translation is so expansive that it is more properly understood as an interpretation rather than straightforward translation. Three things, in particular, will interest us in the Targum's version of the Song of Songs. First, it understands the Song to address Israel's history with its God from the exodus to the future building of the third temple. Second, it immediately understands that history, and, by extension, the Song, in relation to the giving of the Torah at the climax of the exodus.[7] Finally, the third significant element of the Targum's treatment of the Song is in its assumption that the culmination of history will be the reunification of Israel with their God at the time the third temple is complete. We shall see that the two pillars of the theology of love described in part 1 are everywhere presumed in the Targum.

We shall turn to rabbinic midrash in chapter 5 to see another form of early Jewish interpretation of the Song. Again, the authors of midrash presume the centrality of temple and Torah in their interpretations. We shall see that while the Targum understands the Song in the larger literary context of the entire Hebrew Bible, it is in the midrashic collections that are our focus in chapter 5 that this phenomenon becomes remarkably expansive. Furthermore, we shall see the degree to which midrash at one and the same time digresses, yet brings greater clarity to its subject. With deft and stunning insight, it reveals the degree to which scripture can be read as self-referential and, in particular, how the Song of Songs harmonizes with the theology of love in the Hebrew Bible.

In both forms of early Jewish interpretation, we recover not only the degree to which they rely on the theology of love that is the subject of part 1 of our study, but also their attitudes about the sanctity of their literary tradition. For these early interpreters, the Song of Songs, along with the rest of Scripture, originated from the mouth of God. So intimate do they perceive this communication that it is understood in terms of the "kisses of his mouth" of Song of Songs 1:2. Furthermore, we shall observe the degree to which they understand the sensuous beauty of the language of the Song to partake of the divine realities of which it speaks.

In chapter 6 we turn to the earliest extant Christian interpretation of the Song found in Origen. Most important in our discussion of Origen is that he shares with his Jewish contemporaries the high esteem for the Song and its language. Indeed, for Origen, the Song is none other than an account of the great love of the bride (church) for her bridegroom (the Word of God). While Origen's interpretations differ from the Targum and midrash, we shall see that all consider the origins of Scripture and "the

Word" to be divine. In particular, for Origen the Word is associated with the Song, Scripture, and, of course, Jesus as the great lover and redeemer. Perhaps most important in our discussion of the history of interpretation is that both Jews and Christians understand the Song to be about the consummate act of redemption. For Jews, the Song is about the original deliverance during the exodus, while pointing to the deliverance to come with the establishment of the third temple. For Origen and Christians who follow, the Song is about the love for the Word—understood as Jesus. Thus, for Christians, the Song is about the single greatest deliverance of their tradition while simultaneously pointing toward the final deliverance in Jesus' second coming.

Our goal in the following is to establish the parameters of the theology of love in the text of the Hebrew Bible. Secondarily, we will consider the ways in which early interpreters presumed the two main pillars of this theology, temple and Torah, in their understanding of the Song of Songs. What to modern sensibilities may seem an odd reading of the Song turns out to be based on a literary and cultural competence few moderns share with their ancient counterparts.[8] Much of what follows allows us to understand how the Song of Songs came to represent for those who included it in the Bible, a manifesto on God's eternal love and desire for his people, and how, in turn, those devotees invested in the Song the hope that they could return to the halcyon days of their early romance with YHWH.

ABBREVIATIONS

Hebrew Bible

Deut	Deuteronomy
Exod	Exodus
Ezek	Ezekiel
Gen	Genesis
Hos	Hosea
Isa	Isaiah
Jer	Jeremiah
Josh	Joshua
Judg	Judges
Lam	Lamentations
Lev	Leviticus
Nah	Nahum
Num	Numbers
Prov	Proverbs
Ps	Psalms
Qoh	Qohelet/Ecclesiastes
Song	Song of Songs
1 Kgs	1 Kings
1 Sam	1 Samuel
2 Sam	2 Samuel

Apocrypha

Jdt	Judith
Sir	Sirach

Wis   Wisdom of Solomon

Rabbinic Literature

Gen. Rab.   *Genesis Rabbah*
m. Abot   *Mishnah Abot*
m. Yad.   *Mishnah Yadayim*
Pesiq. Rab Kah.   *Pesiqta de Rab Kahana*
Song Rab.   *Song of Songs Rabbah*
Tg.   *Targum*

New Testament

Col   Colossians
1 Cor   1 Corinthians
Eph   Ephesians
Gal   Galatians

Scholarly Publications

AB   Anchor Bible
ACW   Johannes Quasten and Joseph C. Plumpe, eds., *Origen:
                       The Song of Songs Commentary and Homilies*, vol. 26 of
                       *Ancient Christian Writers: The Works of the Fathers in
                       Translation*, trans. R. P. Lawson (New York: Newman,
                       1956)
Bib   *Biblica*
BibInt   *Biblical Interpretation*
BK   *Bibel und Kirche*
BN   *Biblische Notizen*
BRev   *Bible Review*
CBQ   *Catholic Biblical Quarterly*
Did   *Didaskalia*
HBT   *Horizons in Biblical Theology*
HTR   *Harvard Theological Review*

ITS	*Indian Theological Studies*
JAAR	*Journal of the American Academy of Religion*
JBL	*Journal of Biblical Literature*
JNSL	*Journal of Northwest Semitic Languages*
JR	*Journal of Religion*
JSJ	*Journal for the Study of Judaism in the Persian, Hellenistic, and Roman Periods*
JSOT	*Journal for the Study of the Old Testament*
JSOTSup	Journal for the Study of the Old Testament: Supplement Series
LD	Lectio divina
OTL	Old Testament Library
PaVi	*Parole di Vita*
PIBA	Proceedings of the Irish Biblical Association
QD	Quaestiones disputatae
RB	*Revue biblique*
RdT	*Rassegna di teologia*
ResQ	*Restoration Quarterly*
SBLEJL	Society of Biblical Literature Early Judaism and Its Literature
SBLSymS	Society of Biblical Literature Symposium Series
SJOT	*Scandinavian Journal of the Old Testament*
T&H	*Theologica & Historica*
TBT	*The Bible Today*
USQR	*Union Seminary Quarterly Review*
VT	*Vetus Testamentum*
ZAW	*Zeitschrift für die alttestamentliche Wissenschaft*

PART ONE

The Theology of Love in the Hebrew Bible

I accounted to your favor
The devotion of your youth,
Your love as a bride.

—Jeremiah 2:2

CHAPTER ONE

MARRIAGE, APOSTASY, AND DIVORCE: THE PROPHETIC CRITIQUE

Perhaps the most remarkable and discomfiting formulation of the theology of love comes from the prophetic corpus of the Hebrew Bible. Moreover, because the prophets' imagery is so vivid and uncomfortable for moderns, it stands out as among the best-known and most obvious of the theologies of love. The language and imagery of marriage and adultery became central to the prophetic idiom in articulating their understanding of the apostasy of ancient Israel.[1] Our goal in this chapter is to investigate the instances of this motif in the prophetic corpus with an eye to its evolution and development.

We should begin by noting that this motif in the Prophets represents the dissolution of an ideal. To the degree that the Song of Songs represents sexuality at its best, the nearly immediate responsiveness attached to longing, the prophets depict a world in which Israel responds all too quickly to other lovers. In this sense, the prophets share an ideal with the Song of Songs; they merely live through crises in history that suggest to them Israel's unresponsiveness to God.

Hosea

Hosea, who prophesied to the northern kingdom, Israel, in the middle of the eighth century B.C.E., is the first prophet to formulate the marriage/

3

adultery motif, but he likely depends on a theological history that conceptualized the covenant between Israel and God as marriage.[2] That Hosea and prophets who follow him turn to this motif is merely a sign of how badly they perceive the marriage to be going. Indeed, to read a description of how the marriage was in its honeymoon, one need turn no further than Hosea himself. Hosea 2:16-17 reads, "I will persuade her [Israel], lead her in the wilderness, and speak to her heart. . . . She will respond there as in the days of her youth, like the day she arose from Egypt" (AT).[3] Here, Hosea is giving assurances from God that if Israel changes her ways, things can be as good as new. Most important, he presumes the relationship between Israel and God is matrimonial. As we turn to other texts in the Hebrew Bible, we shall see that this presumption is shared across considerable time and in different parts of the biblical text; most important for now is to grasp the remarkable passion embedded in the prophetic critique of Israel's apostasy. The prophets, beginning with Hosea, manage to find a metaphor that communicates their understanding of the desolating effects of Israel's transient and wayward affections.

Hosea wastes no time in describing the status quo as he observes it. In 1:2 he reports that YHWH said to him, "Go, get yourself a wife of whoredom and children of whoredom; for the land will truly stray from YHWH" (AT). In what is known as a classic "prophetic sign act," Hosea is to act in such a way as to represent a theological reality. In this case, by taking a wife of whoredom (*z-n-h*) Hosea's actions suggest that YHWH's own wife (Israel) has become promiscuous.[4] Indeed, that is the message of the first three chapters of Hosea. In chapter 1 he goes on to have three children with Gomer, his promiscuous wife, all given names that are symbolic of God's abandonment of Israel. It is in chapter 2 that we encounter the language and imagery that later prophets seem to know and that provides the means to trace the development of the marriage/adultery motif.

In Hos 2:4-15 we encounter the first formulation of the motif that is generative of the language and imagery that became central to later prophets. Verses 4-15 follow:

> Rebuke your mother, rebuke her—
> For she is not My wife
> And I am not her husband—
> And let her put away her harlotry from her face
> And her adultery from between her breasts.
> Else will I strip her naked

And leave her as on the day she was born:[5]
And I will make her like a wilderness,
Render her like desert land,
And let her die of thirst.
I will also disown her children
For they are now a harlot's brood,
In that their mother has played the harlot,
She that conceived them has acted shamelessly—
Because she thought,
"I will go after my lovers,
Who supply my bread and my water,
My wool and my linen,
My oil and my drink."

Assuredly,
I will hedge up her roads with thorns
And raise walls against her,
And she shall not find her paths.
Pursue her lovers as she will,
She shall not overtake them;
And seek them as she may,
She shall never find them.
Then she will say,
"I will go and return
To my first husband,
For then I fared better than now."
And she did not consider this:
It was I who bestowed on her
The new grain and wine and oil;
I who lavished silver on her
And gold—which they used for Baal.
Assuredly,
I will take back My new grain in its time
And My new wine in its season,
And I will snatch away My wool and My linen
That serve to cover her nakedness.
Now will I uncover her shame
In the very sight of her lovers,
And none shall save her from Me.

And I will end all her rejoicing:
Her festivals, new moons, and sabbaths—
All her festive seasons.
I will lay waste her vines and her fig trees,
Which she thinks are a fee
She received from her lovers;
I will turn them into brushwood,
And beasts of the field shall devour them.
Thus will I punish her
For the days of the Baalim,
On which she brought them offerings;
When, decked with earrings and jewels,
She would go after her lovers,
Forgetting Me

—declares the LORD.

In language that seems perhaps even more out of place in the Bible than that of the Song of Songs, Hosea looses his tirade against the northern kingdom of Israel for its infidelity. As the text of Hosea now stands, this harangue comes on the heels of God's promise that he will gather his children (given symbolic names similar to Hosea's) to safety, and that they are to recite the passage above. For various reasons the originality of 2:1-3 is suspect, but for our purposes we need only concentrate on verses 4-15.

In verse 4, Hosea declares the divorce between God and Israel claiming that she has played the harlot (*z-n-h*) and committed adultery (*n-ʾ-p*). [6] That this is a personal affront is reinforced by the language of intimacy suggested by the use of "face" and "breasts." Hosea no more shrinks from the graphic than does the Song of Songs. As punishment in kind, God threatens to strip (*p-sh-t*) Israel naked (*ʿ-w-r*) like the day she was born and make her like a wilderness. [7] In the biblical idiom, and in particular Hosea's, this language evokes a return to the days before Israel knew YHWH; a time when she was vulnerable and barren. It comes very close to the language of the reversal of creation itself. The uncovering of her nakedness is meant as humiliation; as if to say, "You thought it was so great getting naked with others, how does it feel now?"

Verse 6 states that God will also disown the children of Israel because they are the children of harlotry. That the root *z-n-h* is used twice here reinforces the overload of accusation that this passage is comprised of. Note, as well, that verse 6 provides at least some of the impetus to see

6

verses 1-3 as later additions. Verses 1-3 hardly make sense in the context of the disowning elaborated in verse 6.[8] In verses 7-10 we begin to see more precisely the nature of the charges against Israel. YHWH suggests that she will seek out her lovers who have provisioned her, but YHWH will prevent her from finding them (vv. 7-9). Failing to find her former lovers, she will attempt to return to YHWH. The core of YHWH's complaint comes at the end of verse 10, where he says that it was he who provided her new grain, wine, oil, silver, and gold; the last of which they (Israel) used for Baal. This is the ultimate insult. Baal has been the recipient of Israel's affections and YHWH has been the cuckold.

Hosea provides more invective on this subject in an isolated passage in 4:13-14 where he says:

> They [Israel] sacrifice on the mountaintops
> And offer on the hills,
> Under oaks, poplars, and terebinths
> Whose shade is so pleasant.
> That is why their daughters fornicate [z-n-h]
> And their daughters-in-law commit adultery!
> I will not punish their daughters for fornicating
> Nor their daughters-in-law for committing adultery;
> For they themselves turn aside with whores [z-n-h]
> And sacrifice with prostitutes,
> And a people that is without sense must stumble.

Here, the nature of the infidelity becomes most clear; Israel sacrifices to Baal rather than to the God to whom they owe their very existence. The nature of the accusations in this passage becomes obscure. Some argue that verse 14, in particular, is a reference to an ancient Near Eastern use of cultic prostitution as a means of inducing divine fertility.[9] However we explain the language, it is important to note that here in 4:13-14 Hosea explicitly associates cultic and liturgical apostasy with sexual infidelity, just as he does implicitly in our passage in chapter 2. In addition, note that Hosea apparently extends the marriage/adultery motif that has been restricted to Israel's apostasy and conflates it with real instances of human adultery. It seems that for Hosea, human adultery is as much an affront to Israel's marriage vows to God as is Israel's metaphorical adultery with Baal.

As a result of her infidelity, in 2:11-12 YHWH says that he will take away the things on which Israel used to depend. Most important is that he will take away the wool and linen that cover (*k-s-h*) her nakedness ('-*r-h*) so that he can uncover (*g-l-h*) her shame (*n-b-l*) in the sight of her lovers. Again, we see the punishment in kind that was suggested in verse 5 and that we shall name the nakedness-exposed motif.[10] As we proceed in our analysis of later prophets, we shall see the consistent use of this constellation of language and imagery. Of most importance at this juncture is Hosea's assertion that YHWH is, indeed, a jealous God and Israel will suffer for her actions.

In the last three verses of this indictment, YHWH says that because Israel has forgotten him and gone after Baal, he will end her festivals, new moons, and sabbaths. This amounts to removing the core of Israelite identity. Without these liturgical mileposts, Israel would be lost. It is on those very occasions that Israel renewed its covenantal (marital) vows to its God. From the perspective of this passage, the marriage is broken beyond repair; there is no going back. In attempting to tell Israel the damage she had done to her relationship with YHWH, Hosea must rely on the language of profound personal betrayal. Yet, in the very next passage that concludes chapter 2, YHWH abruptly changes his tone and suggests that he will, again, seduce Israel in the hope that she will respond as in the days of her youth (2:16-17). In a stunning turn of phrase in verse 18, Hosea suggests that Israel can return:

And on that day
—declares the LORD—
You will call [Me] Ishi,
And no more will you call Me Baali.

Hosea puns on the name of Baal to whom Israel had turned.[11] The word is not only a proper noun and the name for the god, it is also a synonym for the word transcribed above as *Ishi*, which means (my) husband. In language that asserts YHWH's desire for renewed intimacy, he claims that Israel shall call him "my husband" and no longer use the term that makes reference to her affair with Baal. Should things go as planned, YHWH says that he will espouse Israel forever and restore the fecundity of her land (vv. 21-25).

As the first of the prophets to employ the marriage/adultery motif, Hosea introduces us to an especially important metaphor in the Hebrew Bible. While Hosea and other prophets concentrate on the broken marriage with which they are confronted, one should not miss the larger point that is articulated so beautifully in Hos 2:16-25. In theory, this started off as a very good marriage, indeed. Implied in that passage is the rich and full fertility that is Israel's endowment from this marriage. Should Israel respond as she did in her youth, all will be forgotten and she will be restored. Importantly, Hosea conceives of the wilderness wandering after the exodus as the honeymoon between God and Israel. The last part of chapter 2 is the expression of the hope that things can be as good as they once were in that first blush of enchantment, romance, and seduction.

With this in mind, it is easy to see how early interpreters of the Song of Songs understood it as a reference to that early stage of their relationship with YHWH. In their ears, the Song represents an extended dialogue during the origins of their love affair with God in the wilderness. Like Hosea's idealized reflections on the honeymoon, interpreters could see the Song of Songs as equally reminiscent of the early days of the relationship.

More important for our purposes in this chapter is that Hosea represents the origin of the prophetic use of the marriage/adultery metaphor. Many prophets who follow him employ similar language and imagery. In the following we trace the three prophets who seem most dependent on Hosea in their use of this primal motif.

Jeremiah

Jeremiah, who prophesied to the southern kingdom, Judah, in the later half of the seventh century B.C.E., employs the imagery of a broken marriage in a number of places. Our goal in the following is to outline those passages and to trace the evolution of the marriage motif. We shall see that while Jeremiah seems dependent on Hosea, or traditions very much like Hosea's, he expands and adapts the motif as well.

Like Hosea, Jeremiah takes aim at two ways in which Israel has broken its vows. Both Judah's apostasy and real human promiscuity are apparently critiqued. Again, as in Hosea, these two are conflated to the degree that they seem inseparable in the prophet's mind and difficult for the interpreter fully to distinguish. The passages that seem to address human promiscuity are found in Jer 5:7-8, 7:9-10, 23:13-14, and 29:23. In 5:7-8 YHWH asks:

> Why should I forgive you?
> Your children have forsaken Me
> And sworn by no-gods.

> When I fed them their fill,
> They committed adultery
> And went trooping to the harlot's house.
> They were well-fed, lusty stallions,
> Each neighing at another's wife.

Addressed to Jerusalem and Judah, this passage apparently indicts the inhabitants of each for forsaking YHWH and committing adultery (*n-ʾ-p*) with harlots (*z-n-h*). Verse 8 reveals the difficulty an interpreter faces in unpacking this metaphor. When Jeremiah suggests that "they were well-fed stallions . . . neighing at another's wife," he employs a variation on a motif that elsewhere is applied to Israel/Judah, writ large, in accusations of apostasy.[12] Again, while this passage seems addressed to conduct between humans, it is very hard to distinguish it from accusations directed more generally toward apostasy. Of most import is that the language is associated with abandoning (ʿ-*z-b*) YHWH.

When we turn to Jer 7:9-10 we are likely on safer ground in claiming that the charge of adultery is of the mundane variety, but even here it is so closely associated with apostasy it is hard to claim a complete differentiation.

> Will you steal and murder and commit adultery [*n-ʾ-p*] and swear falsely, and sacrifice to Baal, and follow other gods whom you have not experienced, and then come and stand before Me in this House which bears My name and say, "We are safe"?—[Safe] to do all these abhorrent things!

This passage comes in the middle of what is known as Jeremiah's "Temple Sermon" in which he tells Judah that they should not rely on false confidence. YHWH makes clear that promises of the covenant are dependent on Judah's behavior. However we understand the reference to adultery (human intercourse or apostasy), it is important that it is, again, associated with sacrifice to Baal and following other gods. That it is found within the Temple Sermon serves to heighten the affront to YHWH— Jeremiah associates adultery, sacrifice to Baal, and apostasy in general with abandoning YHWH and temple etiquette. Furthermore, Jeremiah implies that adultery and apostasy are linked to the defiling of the temple.

In this instance, we see an expansion and variation on the marriage/adultery motif. While Hosea associated sacrifice to Baal and adultery with apostasy, he did not further associate them with the temple because he prophesied to the northern kingdom. It is Jeremiah's proximity to Judah,

10

Jerusalem, and the temple that initiates his association of the motif we are tracing with the temple and its implied defilement. In a later chapter we shall have occasion to trace the significance of this association.

In Jer 23:13-14 we see what is likely the clearest example of the marriage/adultery motif applied to human intercourse. Having said that, it is important to point out that the charge comes in the context of reverence to Baal.

> In the prophets of Samaria
> I saw a repulsive thing:
> They prophesied by Baal
> And led My people Israel astray.
> But what I see in the prophets of Jerusalem
> Is something horrifying:
> Adultery and false dealing.
> They encourage evildoers,
> So that no one turns back from his wickedness.
> To Me they are all like Sodom,
> And [all] its inhabitants like Gomorrah.

In verse 13, Jeremiah suggests that as appalled as YHWH was at the behavior of the northern kingdom of Samaria (to whom Hosea had prophesied), he is even more so with that of the southern kingdom of Judah. Of most significance in this quote is that verses 13 and 14 have parallel structures. In each, the first two lines name the prophets of Samaria and Jerusalem, respectively, and then the expression of YHWH's disgust with what he sees. Importantly, the prophets of Baal in verse 13 are parallel with adultery and false dealing in verse 14. Once again, while the charge of adultery in verse 14 seems to be directed at human intercourse, the structure of these verses seems to associate it with reverence to Baal.

Jeremiah 29:23 comes in the midst of a critique of false prophets in Judah. Significantly, it resonates with Jer 23:13-14 to the degree that false prophets are the target, although here it is only false prophets of the south. Verse 23 is the explanation of why these false prophets (Zedekiah and Ahab) will suffer at the hands of King Nebuchadnezzar of Babylon. It reads:

> Because they did vile things in Israel, committing adultery with the
> wives of their fellows and speaking in My name false words which I had

11

not commanded them. I am He who knows and bears witness—
declares the LORD.

In this passage, we seem finally to have come to a charge of adultery
that applies exclusively to human intercourse. There seems to be little or
no association with apostasy, at least in reference to sacrifice or the temple, but of interest, this act of adultery is associated with speaking falsely
in God's name. It is unclear what this association implies, but it seems
that in this instance we are to understand that YHWH's word is as sacrosanct as his temple. Violation or deviation from either is tantamount to
adultery/apostasy in this verse of Jeremiah.

It is in the passages in chapters 2 and 3 that we see the most explicitly
theological use of the marriage/adultery motif. Here, this motif is used
quite clearly to depict Judah's apostasy.[13]

Jeremiah 2 is an extended diatribe directed at Judah, accusing them of
being a wayward woman. It begins:

> The word of the LORD came to me, saying, Go proclaim to Jerusalem:
>   Thus said the LORD:
> I accounted to your favor
> The devotion of your youth,
> Your love as a bride—
> How you followed Me in the wilderness,
> In a land not sown.

Much like Hosea, Jeremiah imagines the wilderness wanderings that followed the exodus as a honeymoon. Here, YHWH reminisces about the
early devotion of his bride, but it takes little time to discover his complaint. In verses 5-19 Jeremiah continues by claiming that Israel too soon
forgot the benefits of her relationship with YHWH, especially the bounty
that came from the promised land (vv. 5-7). Next, we hear a familiar
refrain: YHWH was abandoned and the prophets prophesied by Baal
(v. 8). Furthermore, YHWH complains that his people have exchanged
its glory for gods that are no gods at all (vv. 9-11). In verse 13 Jeremiah
identifies two wrongs in particular:

> For My people have done a twofold wrong:
> They have forsaken Me, the Font of living waters,
> And hewed them out cisterns, broken cisterns,
> Which cannot even hold water.

Here we encounter new imagery in the marriage/adultery motif. YHWH calls himself the font of living waters and suggests that Judah's apostasy is the equivalent of relying merely on cisterns, which provide no renewable source of water—and leak to boot! This new imagery is hard to appreciate fully in this context, but its significance becomes clearer in the context of the evolution of the imagery of wells and springs in the Hebrew Bible, which we treat in chapter 3 of this study. Within that theological formulation, water eventually comes to be associated with God's presence, especially in Torah. For now we merely point out that Jeremiah has adapted the marriage/adultery motif to imagery that is in keeping with variant traditions of the theology of love in the Hebrew Bible.[14]

In verses 14-19 YHWH asks a series of questions that point out the dangers of relying on Egypt and Assyria as allies and depicts such alliances as forsaking him. It is in verse 20 and following that we, again, find language similar to Hosea's:

> For long ago you broke your yoke,
> Tore off your yoke-bands,
> And said, "I will not work!"
> On every high hill and under every verdant tree,
> You recline as a whore [z-n-h]. . . .
> How can you say, "I am not defiled [t-m-'],
> I have not gone after the Baalim"?
> Look at your deeds in the Valley,
> Consider what you have done!
> Like a lustful she-camel,
> Restlessly running about,
> Or like a wild ass used to the desert,
> Snuffing the wind in her eagerness,
> Whose passion none can restrain,
> None that seek her need grow weary—
> In her season, they'll find her! . . .
> Can a maiden forget her jewels,
> A bride her adornments?
> Yet My people have forgotten Me—
> Days without number.
> How skillfully you plan your way
> To seek out love! (vv. 20, 23-24, 32-33)

In language reminiscent of Hos 4:13, YHWH accuses Judah of play-ing the whore on verdant hills. Note that Hosea accuses Israel of mak-ing sacrifices in the same locale before suggesting that its daughters and daughters-in-law act the whore and commit adultery. We are likely to understand Jeremiah to mean that in "reclining like a whore" Judah, too, is sacrificing to other gods. This notion is supported in verse 23 where Judah is accused of going after the Baalim and thereby becoming defiled. Recall that in Hosea the word *Baal* is understood as a pun on the term for husband (*'-ish*). We are likely to understand Jeremiah, like Hosea, to be associating any act of "whoredom" with apostasy and, in particular, sacrificing to Baal—the god who is not Israel/Judah's real "husband."

Verses 23 and 24 contain an indictment that is familiar from Jer 5:8, but, apparently, used differently. Recall that in Jer 5:8 the charge of being "well-fed . . . stallions, / each neighing at another's wife" seemed to be directed at the inhabitants of Judah in the midst of the accusation of human adultery. Here in Jer 2, the reference is clearly to adultery under-stood explicitly as apostasy and sacrifice to Baal.

Finally, in verse 32, we see a reference, as at the beginning of chapter 2, to the imagery of the honeymoon, where a maiden and bride might cherish the benefits of her new marriage. Verse 33, however, comes back to the point of the entire chapter: having forgotten YHWH, Judah clev-erly plots her next liaison with her lover.

In Jer 3, we find some of the most direct, explicit, and troubling imagery and language associated with the marriage/adultery motif. Chapter 3 begins:

> If a man divorces his wife, and she leaves him and marries another man, can he ever go back to her? Would not such a land be defiled [*kh-n-p*]? Now you have whored [*z-n-h*] with many lovers: can you return to Me?—says the LORD.

In what might be a reference to a law in Deut 24:1-4, YHWH asks whether a wife/land defiled by "whoring" can expect to return to her hus-band. As in many of the texts we have investigated, the implied answer is a resounding no. More to the point, here we get the explicit use of the term for divorce (*sh-l-kh*), albeit prior to the act of promiscuity. Jeremiah 3:2-4 continues and intensifies the charges:

> Look up to the bare heights, and see:
> Where have they not lain with you [*sh-g-l*]?[15]
> You waited for them on the roadside
> Like a bandit in the wilderness.
> And you defiled [*kh-n-p*] the land
> With your whoring [*z-n-h*] and debauchery.
> And when showers were withheld
> And the late rains did not come,
> You had the brazenness of a street woman [*z-n-h*],
> You refused to be ashamed.
> Just now you called to Me, "Father!
> You are the Companion of my youth."

In familiar language, Jeremiah piles on the accusations. In the reference to the "bare heights," we should likely understand sacrifice to other gods. It is immediately associated with sexual infidelity that can be translated in obscene language (see n. 15). The term *sh-g-l* in Hebrew is clearly to be understood in such a light and may well imply, as in English, both the notion of sexual intercourse and being taken advantage of at the same time.[16] More important, this is the tone of the impassioned language in this part of Jeremiah. Again, we see the association of defilement of the land with sexual misconduct, suggesting that the land, like a woman, is defiled by adultery. As in other examples of the marriage/adultery motif, fertility is associated with proper relations with YHWH and barrenness with the breaking of the bonds with him. Note, too, that this time of fertility is associated with the reference to YHWH as Judah's "companion of my youth." Again, as in other examples of the motif, implied is the early stages of the relationship when things went well.

In Jer 3:6-13 we find a new variation on the marriage/adultery motif (Israel and Judah are depicted as sisters) that will be picked up and expanded by Ezekiel. Here Jeremiah begins with a reference to the northern kingdom of Israel:

The LORD said to me in the days of King Josiah[17]: Have you seen what Rebel Israel did, going to every high mountain and under every leafy tree, and whoring [*z-n-h*] there? I thought: After she has done all these things, she will come back to Me. But she did not come back; and her sister, Faithless Judah, saw it. I noted: Because Rebel Israel had committed adultery [*n-ʾ-p*], I cast her off [*sh-l-kh*] and handed her a bill of divorce [*s-p-r k-r-t*]; yet her sister, Faithless Judah, was not afraid—she too went and whored [*z-n-h*]. Indeed, the land was defiled [*kh-n-p*] by her casual immorality, as she committed adultery [*n-ʾ-p*] with stone and with wood. And after all that, her sister, Faithless Judah, did not return to Me wholeheartedly, but insincerely—declares the LORD.

In verses 11-13 YHWH declares a hope of restoration for Israel in light of the events just recited. Yet, in Jer 3:6-10 we see the by now familiar vocabulary and imagery: the high mountain, leafy tree, whoring, adultery and divorce. Clearly, this constellation of vocabulary signals that Judah's faithlessness comes in the form of apostasy, as did Israel's. New here, however, is the notion that Judah should have learned from her sister's experience. The text implies that she should have seen in her sister, Israel, an object lesson. Whoring and adultery in high places compose worship of other gods and initiate divorce proceedings on the part of YHWH. That Jer 3:11-13 offers hope of restoration to Israel is followed in verses 14 and 15 with a call to YHWH's "rebellious children" (both Israel and Judah) to turn back. As bleak as the situation is, it appears that there is still hope that the relationship might be redeemed. Like Hos 2:16-25, Jeremiah follows the description of a marriage in total dissolution with the hope that things can be made right.

While Jer 3 comprises perhaps his fullest and most articulate version of the marriage/adultery motif—one that, as noted, seems to influence Ezekiel, we need to consider one last passage from the book of Jeremiah that continues a motif from Hosea and is, again, elaborated more fully in Ezekiel.

In Jer 13:22-27 he includes the nakedness-exposed motif first seen in Hos 2:5, 11, and 12; but it is Jeremiah's language that seems to become part of the formulaic usage of the motif. In the early parts of Jer 13 he complains that Judah has made foreign alliances and apparently lost any real autonomy. Starting in verse 22, he continues:

> And when you ask yourself,
> "Why have these things befallen me?"
> It is because of your great iniquity [ʿ-w-n]
> that your skirts [*sh-w-l*] are lifted [*g-l-h*] up,
> Your limbs [ʿ-q-b] exposed [*kh-m-s*].
> Can the Cushite change his skin,
> Or a leopard his spots?
> Just as much can you do good,
> Who are practiced in doing evil!

So I will scatter you like straw that flies
Before the desert wind.
This shall be your lot,
Your measured portion from Me
>   —declares the LORD.

Because you forgot Me
And trusted falsehood,
I in turn will lift [*kh-s-p*] your skirts [*sh-w-l*] over your face
And your shame [*q-l-h*] shall be seen.
I behold your adulteries [*n-ʾ-p*],
Your lustful neighing [*ts-h-l*],
Your unbridled depravity [*z-n-h*], your vile acts
On the hills of the countryside.
Woe to you, O Jerusalem,
Who will not be clean!
How much longer shall it be?

Like Hosea, Jeremiah suggests that the punishment for "whoring and adultery" on the part of Judah will be in kind. While the Hebrew roots *z-n-h* and *n-ʾ-p*, for "whore" and "adultery" respectively, are consistent in both Jeremiah and Hosea, Jeremiah shares only one other root, *g-l-h* (for lift up or uncover), with Hosea (2:12) in what are strikingly similar images. As noted before, this expansion of the nakedness-exposed motif seems to influence later uses. Most important for now is to review the marriage/adultery motif as it has emerged in Hosea and Jeremiah.

Hosea and Jeremiah both depict apostasy, worshiping or sacrificing to other gods, as adultery. In both prophets we see that it is hard to distinguish between real acts of human sexual intercourse and metaphorical religious forms of apostasy. This confusion is because in nearly every instance the two prophets employ what seem to be references to human sexual activity in the context of worshipping foreign gods. More to the point, Jeremiah, like Hosea, imagines a good marriage gone bad. Both look to the early days of the marriage, associated with the wilderness wanderings, as the ideal. Both prophets also hold out hope that as bad as things have become, there might be a reconciliation.

At this juncture of our study there are a few particularly salient issues that have emerged. First, we see in Jeremiah an elaboration and amplification of the nakedness-exposed motif. Second, the prophets depict the apostasy of Israel/Judah consistently in the language of whoring and adultery. This marks the deep personal insult they perceive is done to YHWH in Israel's or Judah's wayward religious life. In particular, Baal comes in for the greatest criticism. This is clearly because the Canaanite deity attracted many of YHWH's followers historically and may be because the term *Baal* could also be used as the term for "husband." Recall Hos 2:18 and the pun where YHWH says "You will call [Me] Ishi, and no more will you call Me Baali." The consistent use and critique of the name Baal is likely because of historical realities but also because of the way in which the term serves to suggest to whom Israel and Judah are really married and to whom they owe their allegiance. The third issue is related to the second and became most clear, so far, in the passage from Jer 7, known as the Temple Sermon. Implied in the association of adultery, sacrifice to Baal, and the temple itself is that some kind of defilement takes place. While Jer 7 does not specifically state it, it would appear that the more general understanding of adultery as the defilement of the land would suggest the defilement of the temple as well. Jeremiah never clearly associates defilement of adultery and the land with the temple; however, we shall see later in this study that just such an association becomes paramount in later writers of the Hebrew Bible.

Finally, as noted above, consistent in the marriage/adultery motif is its association with fertility when the marriage is going well. In Hosea and Jeremiah we see references to the past, in particular the wilderness wanderings and delivery into the promised land, in light of how fecund Israel was (as a land and people). Indeed, it seems the great insult to YHWH is not that Israel celebrates its fertility or sexuality, but only that it celebrates it with the wrong god(s)! For the prophets, the nubility of Israel is properly to be directed only toward the lover of her youth.

Nahum

Nahum prophesied at a time contemporaneous with Jeremiah, ca. 650–612 B.C.E., but, unlike the other prophets who are the focus of this study, employs part of the marriage/adultery motif to the foreign nation Assyria and, specifically, to its capital, Nineveh.[18] Nahum lived in a period that saw the weakening of the Assyrians and the concomitant ascendancy of Babylonia. Nahum represents the delight taken among Israelites that this formidable foe was in its last days. He begins in chapter 1 by asserting that YHWH does not tolerate his enemies and implying that he is about to take revenge on Assyria. In chapter 2 Nahum continues by reassuring Judah that "never again shall scoundrels invade you" (2:1). Filled with martial imagery, Nahum depicts Nineveh in the panic of utter defeat. Nahum finally turns his invective toward Nineveh in chapter 3 where we encounter his use of the nakedness-exposed part of the marriage/adultery motif.

Ah, city of crime,
Utterly treacherous,
Full of violence,
Where killing never stops!

Crack of whip
And rattle of wheel,
Galloping steed
And bounding chariot!
Charging horsemen,
Flashing swords,
And glittering spears!
Hosts of slain
And heaps of corpses,
Dead bodies without number—
They stumble over bodies.
Because of the countless harlotries [*z-n-h*] of the harlot [*z-n-h*],
The winsome mistress of sorcery,
Who ensnared nations with her harlotries [*z-n-h*]
And peoples with her sorcery,
I am going to deal with you
                         —declares the LORD of Hosts.
I will lift [*g-l-h*] up your skirts [*sh-w-l*] over your face
And display your nakedness [*'-r-h*] to the nations
And your shame [*q-l-h*] to kingdoms.
I will throw loathsome things over you
And disfigure you
And make a spectacle of you.
All who see you will recoil from you
and will say,
"Nineveh has been ravaged!"
Who will console her?
Where shall I look for
Anyone to comfort you? (vv. 1-7)

Nahum's rage at Nineveh is as obvious as it is well deserved. Of most interest, of course, is the application of the nakedness-exposed motif. Here we encounter the language that we have seen in other prophets, including the charge of being a harlot or whore (*z-n-h*) and the threat of payment in kind through exposing Nineveh's nakedness. Note that in verse 5 we have language so close to Jer 13:22 and 26 that it suggests Nahum's dependence on Jeremiah or at least on traditions familiar to both. Below, the structure of the pertinent parts of the verses in question make clear the remarkable similarities among them. Nahum 3:5 appears first followed by Jer 13:22 below it and Jer 13:26 on the last line. I have added space between words merely to reveal the verbal correspondence among the three.

> *wegilleti shulayikh ʿal-panayikh,*
> > *wehar'eti goyim maʿrekh, umamlakhot*   *qelonekh*
> *niglu*   *shulayikh*
> *khasafti*   *shulayikh ʿal-panayikh, wenir'ah*   *qelonekh*

Nahum's "I will lift up your skirts over your face" (*wegilleti shulayikh ʿal-panayikh*) and Jeremiah's language in 13:22 "Your skirts are lifted up" (*niglu shulayikh*) share the use of the verbal root *g-l-h*, to lift. Nahum merely uses the Piel active form of the root while Jeremiah employs it in the passive Niphal. Clearly, both Nahum and Jeremiah use identical terms for "your skirts" (*shulayikh*) from the root *sh-w-l*.

Jeremiah 13:26 reveals the closest verbal parallels with Nahum and is the reason to suspect some genetic link between them. Note that in the first part of each only the verb differs. Jeremiah 13:26 uses the root *kh-s-p*, translated "lift" but maybe better translated "strip" or "strip off." More to the point, comparison of the remainder of the first parts of Nah 3:5 and Jer 13:26 show the identical "your skirts over your face" (*shulayikh ʿal-panayikh*).

The latter part of Nah 3:5 seems to be an expansion and variation on the version found in the last part of Jer 13:26. Jeremiah merely records "your shame shall be seen" (*wenir'ah qelonekh*) while Nahum records "I will display your nakedness to the nations and your shame to kingdoms" (*wehar'eti goyim maʿrekh, umamlakhot qelonekh*). Clearly, both use the root for sight *r-'-h*, but Jeremiah uses it in the passive Niphal while Nahum employs the causative Hiphil. Nahum's expansion on the simple exposure of "shame" found in Jer 13:26 may be because of his awareness that the nakedness-exposed motif typically has nakedness exposed, rather than shame. If this is the case, Nahum may represent a filling out of a shorter version like Jeremiah's in order to bring his own version more in line with the standard formula. In addition, note that Nahum adds specificity to the formula in Jeremiah by changing the verb from passive to active and by naming those to whom YHWH will reveal both the nakedness and the shame. Whatever the relationship between Nah 3 and Jer 13, that they have such similar phrasing is remarkable.

As noted above, this constellation of language and imagery, used in such consistent ways, suggests that Nahum and Jeremiah are dependent on the same tradition. Further, that they both echo yet refine Hosea's nakedness-exposed motif in similar ways reinforces such a suspicion. Notably, Nahum's employment of this motif is distinct from Hosea and Jeremiah in an important detail. The explicit language and imagery of adultery (*n-ʾ-p*) is entirely absent for obvious reasons. While Israel and Judah were understood to be married to YHWH, clearly Nineveh was not. This may be the most striking thing about Nahum's use of the nakedness-exposed motif. He has adapted it to a use that would, in all likelihood, have been jarring to the native hearer. What might Nahum have been trying to do in employing such a remarkable variation on the motif? Several answers suggest themselves. First, the motif is likely well known enough that he would have attracted considerable attention in using it. The motif becomes all the more riveting when applied to Nineveh. Moreover, while Hosea and Jeremiah (especially the latter's critique of "Rebel Israel" in ch. 3) saw Assyria as among the assorted lovers to whom YHWH's lover had turned, now Nahum delivers a kind of double payment in kind. Not only will Assyria suffer the consequences once reserved for Israel, like Israel it will be the payment in kind that comprises nakedness exposed. Assyria, to whom Israel once exposed her nakedness by choice and then as punishment, will now have its own nakedness exposed. YHWH will, as it were, cause Nineveh to hoist its skirts with its own "petard."

Whatever the rhetorical strategy that lay behind Nahum's use of the nakedness-exposed motif, one can hardly escape the sense that it comes with unintended consequences.[19] In Hosea and Jeremiah, Israel/Judah are understood as YHWH's adulterous wives among whose lovers Assyria could be included. The implication, of course, is that Assyria and its religious practices were, like Baal, the male lovers to whom YHWH's wife had turned. Curiously, in Nahum, the gender of Nineveh is reversed.

Now she is conceived as a whore or harlot who will suffer the payment in kind for her actions. In the creative world of biblical metaphor, such unintended consequences are to be expected, but this instance is especially intriguing: to the degree that Nineveh is understood to be female, Israel must be understood as among her potential male suitors.

Ezekiel

Ezekiel prophesied in exile after the defeat of Jerusalem ca. 598 B.C.E. and the destruction of the temple in ca. 587 B.C.E. He likely continued his prophetic mission until around 575 B.C.E. Unlike Hosea or Jeremiah, who saw impending disaster, Ezekiel writes from the perspective of its consequences. Here, we get the postmortem on the nation of Judah. We find in Ezekiel two chapters, 16 and 23, devoted to the marriage/adultery motif, each of which is an elaboration of Jeremiah's "wanton sisters" motif of chapter 3. In addition to elaborating on the notion that Israel and Judah were wayward sisters, Ezekiel also employs the language, imagery, and passion common to previous examples of the marriage/ adultery motif.

Ezekiel 16 comprises sixty-three verses dedicated to the notion that Jerusalem has played the harlot and committed adultery. YHWH begins by recalling the origins of his relationship with Judah, depicted as a child abandoned in an open field. Here there is no overt reference to the exodus or wilderness wanderings but, still, a recollection of the early, innocent days of the past.[20] In 16:7-8 YHWH states:

> You were still naked and bare when I passed by you [again] and saw that your time for love had arrived. So I spread My robe over you and covered your nakedness, and I entered into a covenant with you by oath— declares the LORD God; thus you became Mine.

Here we see, proleptically, the opposite of the "nakedness exposed" motif. It was part of the divine favor, indeed through the espousal of Judah in covenant with YHWH, that Judah's nakedness was covered. In Ezek 16:9-14 we hear of all the benefits that accrued to Judah through her close relations with YHWH.

In verse 15, however, we see that things have changed. YHWH accuses Judah of taking advantage of her beauty and fame, playing the harlot (*z-n-h*), and pouring out her favors (*z-n-h*) on passersby. He goes on to accuse her of taking the gold and silver objects he had given her and making phallic images with which she fornicated (*z-n-h*) (v. 17). Furthermore, YHWH claims that Judah has employed the bounty of the harvest—flour, oil, and honey—for the purpose of offerings to other gods (v. 19). Worst of all, YHWH says that she has sacrificed her children, the gifts of YHWH, to other gods (vv. 20, 21). In verses 23-30 the accusations keep piling up until YHWH suggests that Judah's behavior does not even rise to the standard of a whore (*z-n-h*), who at least gets paid for her services. Judah has been adulterous (*n-ʾ-p*) in that she has cheated on her husband and even bribed her lovers to sleep with her (vv. 31-34).

In Ezek 16:35-43 YHWH details the consequences of Judah's effrontery. For offering her nakedness to her lovers, he declares that he will assemble all of her lovers and "expose [*g-l-h*] your nakedness [ʿ*-r-h*] to them, and they shall see [*r-ʾ-h*] all your nakedness [ʿ*-r-h*]" (v. 37). Like Jer 13:22 and Nah 3:5, Ezekiel employs the verb "to lift or expose" (*g-l-h*), but here it is not the skirts that are lifted, but rather the nakedness that is exposed. Also like Jer 13:26 and Nah 3:5, the verb "to see" is employed, but here it is, again, her nakedness (ʿ*-r-h*) that the former lovers will see rather than her shame (*q-l-h*). Of interest is that Ezekiel employs the identical word, including its inflection, for nakedness that we saw in Hos 2:11. Clearly, the phraseology is altered, but it is obvious that Ezekiel understands the nakedness-exposed motif to be part of the larger marriage/adultery motif. The charge of adultery is found again in verse 38. At the end YHWH's threat in 35-43 he says that all of this will happen because Judah "did not remember the days of [her] youth." Again, the constellation of imagery and language that compose the marriage/adultery motif is employed in the wake of the dissolution of the marriage brought on by Judah's forgetfulness and apostasy.

Ezekiel 16:44-63 takes up the sister motif that we first saw in Jer 3. Here, YHWH identifies Judah's older sister as Samaria or the northern kingdom of Israel. An addition to Jeremiah's account of the sisters is Ezekiel's identification of Judah's younger sister Sodom. Clearly, the association of Judah and Israel with Sodom, famous for its immorality, reveals the depths to which Ezekiel perceives the two nations have sunk. Ezekiel does not suggest that Judah should have learned its lesson from her sisters but, rather, that Judah's sins make her sisters look righteous (vv. 47-52)! Like Jer 3 and Hos 2, Ezek 16 ends with reassurance that Samaria, Sodom, and Judah will be restored. YHWH promises to honor the covenant he made with them in the days of their youth in order to reconcile the broken marriage (vv. 53-63).

Ezekiel 23 comprises an extended treatment of the sister motif in its entirety.[21] Here, YHWH identifies Samaria as Oholah ("tent") and Jerusalem as Oholibah ("my tent is in her"). We will consider the significance of these names later, for now it is our task to see how Ezekiel employs the wanton sister motif a second time. YHWH begins by claiming that there were two sisters who, in their youth, played the whore in Egypt (vv. 1-3). He then names them in verse 4 before turning to the older sister's, Oholah's, behavior in verses 5-10.

As in other examples of the sister variation of the marriage/adultery motif, YHWH accuses Samaria, Oholah, of whoring while she was his. In particular, YHWH points out her "bestowing her favors (z-n-h)" on the Assyrians through which she defiled (t-m-ʾ) herself (vv. 5-9). As a consequence, YHWH declares:

> Therefore I delivered her into the hands of her lovers, into the hands of the Assyrians after whom she lusted. They exposed [g-l-h] her nakedness [ʿ-r-h]; they seized her sons and daughters, and she herself was put to the sword. And because of the punishment inflicted upon her, she became a byword among women.

At the beginning of verse 10 we have the same vocabulary used in Ezek 16:36 with its same associations to Jeremiah, Nahum, and Hosea discussed above. In a slight variation, it is not YHWH who exposes Oholah's nakedness but her Assyrian lovers.

In verse 11, YHWH turns his harangue on Oholibah, claiming that her behavior was worse than her sister Oholah. Not only did she lust after and act the whore with the Assyrians, and thereby defile (t-m-ʾ) herself, she then turned her lust toward the Babylonians (vv. 11-16). Verses 17 and 18 contain the main complaint against Oholibah:

> So the Babylonians came to her for lovemaking and defiled [t-m-ʾ] her with their whoring [z-n-h]; and she defiled [t-m-ʾ] herself with them until she turned from them in disgust. She flaunted [g-l-h] her harlotries [z-n-h] and exposed [g-l-h] her nakedness [ʿ-r-h], and I turned from her in disgust, as I had turned disgusted from her sister.

From Ezekiel's perspective, Oholibah's actions represent an even worse offense than her sister's. Like Oholah, Oholibah's liaisons with Assyria and then Babylonia, in turn, result in her defilement. Unlike Oholah, whose nakedness was exposed by her lover, Oholibah exposes her own nakedness. We are likely to see in this even more immodest behavior and greater offense. As the end of verse 18 states, the result of the sisters' actions is that YHWH turns in disgust from both. While we have no explicit language of divorce, clearly YHWH is displeased.

Ezekiel 23:19-35 continues the complaint and turns to the consequences for such wanton behavior. YHWH will summon the Babylonians, Assyrians, and all of Oholibah's former lovers to attack and destroy her. In verse 26 he claims that they will "strip" (*p-sh-t*) her of her clothes, and in verse 29 that they will "leave you naked (*ʿ-w-r*) and bare (*ʿ-r-h*); your naked (*ʿ-r-h*) whoredom (*z-n-h*), wantonness (*z-m-m*), and harlotry (*z-n-h*) will be exposed (*g-l-h*)." Here we find the highest concentration of the vocabulary of the nakedness exposed that we have encountered. The overload of the language is likely meant to convey YHWH's utter frustration and fury. Now the payment in kind will be delivered, as it was with Oholah, by Oholibah's former lovers. In verse 30, YHWH declares, "These things shall be done to you for your harlotries (*z-n-h*) with the nations, for defiling (*t-m-ʾ*) yourself with their fetishes."

Verse 36 records YHWH's request that Ezekiel arraign and bring charges against Oholah and Oholibah. It is only in verse 37 that we finally see that adultery (*n-ʾ-p*) is the first charge brought against them. In addition, YHWH accuses them of offering as sacrifices the children they bore him.[22] YHWH continues by claiming that in sacrificing their children, Oholah and Oholibah defiled (*t-m-ʾ*) his sanctuary (*m-q-d-sh*) and profaned (*kh-l-l*) his sabbaths (v. 38). We have seen in other examples of the marriage/adultery motif the notion that defilement is associated with Israel/Judah's apostasy. Jeremiah 3:1 associates adultery with defilement of the land itself. Further, we suggested in the discussion of Jer 7:9-10 that he implies that Judah's adultery and sacrificing to Baal defiles the temple but, again, he does not specifically say so. Here in Ezek 23:38 we see a direct association of Israel's and Judah's adultery with their own defilement and, more important, the defiling of the temple. This last point must await fuller discussion in the conclusion to this chapter.

In Ezek 23:40-47, YHWH wraps up his indictment by pointing out that Oholah and Oholibah primped to meet their new lovers (v. 40), laid out YHWH's incense and oil as enticement (v. 41), and allowed their lovers to come to them as one comes to a whore (*z-n-h*) (v. 44). In verse 45, YHWH declares that righteous men will punish the sisters for their adultery. Finally, YHWH ends his tirade with the prediction of the death of Oholah and Oholibah, the elimination of idolatry and wickedness from the land, and the assertion that through this punishment, they will know that he is the Lord God. In exile, Ezekiel makes no facile prediction of reconciliation.

Summary of the Prophetic Critique

Presuming a good marriage gone bad, each of the prophets discussed above, with the exception of Nahum, laments the dissolution of a relationship that, when going well, results in fertility and well-being. Employing the language and imagery of adultery to make the charge of apostasy personalizes the relationship and the offense. While the marriage/adultery motif usually ends with some reassurance that rapprochement is possible, it is not a consistent element. Ezekiel 23, for example, lacks any such reassurance, while chapter 16 suggests things will work out in the end. That the prophets rely on the marriage/adultery motif suggests that they desperately want to provide YHWH with good reason for Israel's misfortunes and, at the same time, preserve the fantasy that, at the end of the day, they had control of the world they lived in. From this perspective, fidelity would have guaranteed their safety. Historical circumstances suggest that the fate of Israel and Judah was sealed but, in moments of crisis, defeat, and devastation, they strove to understand their bitter disappointment and to articulate the hope that YHWH would rekindle the affair.

More important for our discussion of the theology of love, we have seen the evolution of the marriage/adultery motif that comes to fullest expression in Ezekiel. Of interest here is the growing link between defilement of adultery and defilement of the temple. While Ezekiel provides the most explicit formulation of this linkage, we saw that Jeremiah seems to presume it and that Hosea, by associating adultery with apostasy (as cultic infidelity), presumes the link between defilement of adultery and defilement of the cult. In the constellation of imagery and vocabulary that are comprised in this ideology, the temple, subject to defilement as much as Judah (understood as a woman), takes on the characteristics of a woman. Reinforcing this assertion is that the names for the two sisters in Ezek 23, *Oholah* and *Oholibah*, mean "tent" and "my tent is in her," respectively. The root ('*-h-l*) of both names is used in several instances in the

Hebrew Bible to refer to the tent either confounded with or merely associated with the tabernacle. It is likely that in Ezekiel's naming of the two sisters he implies that to the degree that they are defiled, so is the tabernacle/temple. We will see that this notion, while remaining implicit in the prophetic material considered thus far, is elaborated in the temple-as-woman motif to which we turn in chapter 2. It was this emergent linkage between apostasy, adultery, and consequent defilement with the temple that led to conceiving of the temple as one of the two main conduits of the theology of love in the Second Temple period.

THE TEMPLE, WOMEN, AND WOMBS

A s we saw in the last chapter, the theology of love in the Prophets presumes a matrimonial relationship with all its related complications between God and Israel. It is our goal in this chapter to consider the permutations and adaptations of the temple-as-woman motif in the Hebrew Bible. As we shall see, this motif seems to pick up and elaborate on the prophetic trend toward associating the temple with a woman's womb. In this instance, we shall start with Ezekiel's account that comes on the heels of his depiction of Oholah and Oholibah in chapter 23. After gaining a better understanding of the metaphor at work in Ezek 24, we shall turn to other texts to investigate the ways in which it evolved and was adapted in different historical contexts.

Ezekiel 24:1-14 comprises a warning to Jerusalem and by extension Judah that the Babylonian siege that had begun that day would result in utter destruction. Ezekiel goes on to depict the siege as a purifying fire and a caldron meant to remove all uncleanness. YHWH is recorded to say, "You shall never be clean again until I have satisfied My fury upon you." Of interest for our purposes is the passage that follows in Ezek 24:15-27. It begins with Ezekiel's report that YHWH came to him and said:

> O mortal, I am about to take away the delight [*m-kh-m-d*] of your eyes from you through pestilence; but you shall not lament or weep or let your tears flow.

Ezekiel is further instructed not to observe mourning for the dead (v. 17). Verse 18 informs us that in the evening Ezekiel's wife died. The next morning, people inquire what Ezekiel's actions portend (v. 19). Ezekiel's answer comes in verses 21-24.

> "Tell the House of Israel: Thus said the Lord GOD: 'I am going to dese-crate [*kh-l-l*] My Sanctuary [*m-q-d-sh*], your pride and glory, the delight [*m-kh-m-d*] of your eyes and the desire of your heart; and the sons and daughters you have left behind shall fall by the sword. And Ezekiel shall become a portent for you: you shall do just as he has done, when it hap-pens; and you shall know that I am the Lord GOD.' "

After explaining the significance of his actions, YHWH addresses Ezekiel again in verse 25 and tells him that on the day he removes the temple from Jerusalem, Ezekiel's voice shall be restored.

As a prophetic sign-act, the message of Ezek 24:15-27 is clear. Just as Ezekiel will lose the delight of his eyes, so, too, will Jerusalem. Like the marriage/adultery motif, this sign-act presumes the marriage metaphor, but with a difference. Whereas in the former God was understood to be married to Israel or Judah, here it is implied that God's spouse is not the people but the temple.[1] At least part of an adequate explanation for this alteration lies in the phenomenon of synecdoche by which terms can be used either in the relation of part for whole or whole for part. The same phenomenon explains the use of Israel/Samaria and Judah/Jerusalem for the people thereof. While synecdoche explains this alteration in part, it does not fully reveal the significance of the association of the temple with Ezekiel's wife.

One might turn to Hosea for an example of this motif since in that text Hosea's wife represents God's spouse just as Ezekiel's wife does in Ezek 24. Again, while this analogy helps to understand, in part, the reason Ezekiel may have used this motif, it does not fully explain the fact that the tem-ple is now understood as YHWH's spouse and not the people in general.

An adequate answer to why Ezekiel's sign-act represents the temple as a woman leads in two main directions. The first relies on our investiga-tion in the last chapter and the second is the focus of this chapter. Recall that in chapter 1 of this study we noted the emergent association of defilement of Israel/Judah (as God's spouse) with the defilement of the temple. While this association seemed inchoate and nascent in Jer 7, it seemed to come relatively close to full articulation in Ezek 23:38. In the latter, Oholah and Oholibah are accused of defiling (*t-m-'*) the temple

(m-q-d-sh) and profaning (kh-l-l) the Sabbath. While the immediate reference was to child sacrifice, that the text refers to both sisters defiling themselves (t-m-$^{}$) earlier in the chapter suggests a close association between their defilement and the temple's. This implies that underlying Ezekiel's message in 23:38 is the association of women and their defilement with the temple and its defilement. Adding to this impression, recall that the names *Oholah* and *Oholibah* mean, respectively, "my tent" and "my tent is in her." It seems likely that Ezekiel's naming of the sisters and their subsequent defilement is meant to represent the defilement of the tabernacle/temple as well. Given this context, it seems that Ezek 24 is a natural extension of his assumptions in chapter 23, but made explicit. From this perspective, the temple is understood as a woman.

To some degree the evolution of the marriage/adultery motif traced in chapter 1 of this study explains Ezekiel's use of the motif wherein the temple equals a woman, but there is a larger context in which to understand this motif. In the remainder of this chapter we trace other places in the Hebrew Bible in which this motif is presumed or articulated. In some instances the texts we study are not only explicit in this association but also represent considerable development and adaptation of it.

Lamentations

The book of Lamentations, among the texts we shall focus on in this chapter, was written at a time closest to Ezekiel. Produced in the wake of the destruction of the temple in ca. 587 B.C.E., the book comprises an extended lamentation in the form of the question, *How?* More to the point, *How had this happened? How could it be that the temple was destroyed, Jerusalem sacked, and the literati and political elite exiled?* Credited to Jeremiah but in actuality written anonymously, the text signals both how important the temple was to ancient Israel and how devastating was its loss. Like Ezekiel and other texts in the Hebrew Bible, Lamentations understood God's presence to reside in the temple. With his home destroyed and his people in exile, the great challenge of the period of the exile and beyond was to reconceive God's presence in the world.[2]

Comprising five chapters, the book of Lamentations represents the shock of the conquest of Jerusalem and the loss of the temple. In heartbreaking language and images the book repeatedly points out the suffering of the city and the anxiety over its culpability. Here the city, like the temple, is understood as a woman. In this case the city, personified as a woman, continually seeks to understand how this could have happened.[3] In chapter 1, Jerusalem is referred to in the third person. Verse 1 reads:

> Alas!
> Lonely sits the city
> Once great with people!
> She that was great among the nations
> Is become like a widow;
> The princess among states
> Is become a thrall.

It is in the description of Jerusalem in verses 9 and 10 that we encounter language and imagery familiar from our previous analyses.

> Her uncleanness [*t-m-ʾ*] clings to her skirts [*sh-w-l*].
> She gave no thought to her future;
> She has sunk appallingly,
> With none to comfort [*n-kh-m*] her.—
> See, O LORD, my misery;
> How the enemy jeers!
> The foe has laid hands
> On everything dear [*m-kh-m-d*] to her.
> She has seen her Sanctuary [*m-q-d-sh*]
> Invaded by nations
> Which You have denied admission
> Into Your community.

While at first glance this passage may seem only remotely related to the temple-as-woman motif, it is important on a number of counts. Simply the recurrence of language that appears in the prophetic idiom of the marriage/adultery motif should grab our attention. That it is used in conjunction with language of the temple in this way is doubly fascinating. To begin with verse 9, we see the same word used for "defilement" in the prophetic texts when they refer to the whoring and adultery of Israel. Clearly, the terminology for either of those two forms of promiscuity is absent in our verse, but that the term for defilement appears in the same verse with the term *skirts* suggests that the prophetic idiom informs this usage. If this is true, Lamentations represents a variation on the prophetic motif. In the prophets, the fact that Israel/Judah had defiled herself through her liaisons with others led to the punishment of what we called the nakedness-exposed motif. Recall that in Nah 3:5 we saw the notion that Nineveh's skirts would be lifted over her head to reveal her nakedness. This appears to be a variant of Jer 13 in which the skirts are lifted to reveal either her limbs (v. 22) or her shame (v. 26). In Lam 1:9 we may be meant to see a shorthand reference to the prophetic idiom but we cannot be sure. More to the point, the association of defilement with skirts is reminiscent of the prophetic critique.

An important issue arises with the use of the term *skirts* (*sh-w-l*) in this passage. Outside its use in Jeremiah, Nahum, and here in Lamentations, it is always used in reference to clothing worn in the temple. In Exodus it is used in describing the vestments that Aaron is to wear in the tabernacle while engaged in priestly duties (Exod 28:33, 34; 39:24, 25, 26). In Isaiah's temple vision, found in 6:1, the term refers to the robes that YHWH wears. Perhaps among all the uses of the term in the Hebrew Bible, Nahum's is most difficult to understand, but the likelihood that he has adapted his nakedness-exposed motif to a foreign city may explain the incongruity. At any rate, Jeremiah's use may suggest that the term was heavily loaded with associations to the temple and vestments appropriate to it; its use became all the more shocking when associated with exposed nakedness. We cannot be sure that Jeremiah or Lamentations implies an association with the temple with this term, but its use in the latter, in verse 9, followed as it is by the invasion of the temple by unauthorized visitors, is highly suggestive indeed. This brings us to the imagery and language of verse 10.

Note that verse 10 begins by claiming that the foe has "laid hands on everything that is dear to her." In the word for "dear" (*m-kh-m-d*) we have the identical term that Ezekiel uses in reference to his wife and the temple (24:16, 21).[4] Given its location in the constellation of language of verses 9-10, it is a least prudent to consider the possibility that Ezekiel's usage is echoed deliberately. Whatever conclusion we draw, the last part of verse 10 is most significant for our study.

In a reference to the invasion of the Babylonians and their taking of the temple, the text states: "She has seen her Sanctuary / Invaded by nations / Which You have denied admission / Into Your community." Clearly, this is an account that anywhere in the biblical corpus would be understood as the defilement of the temple. Indeed, this may be the presumption that informs the use of the term for defilement (*t-m-'*) in verse 9. More important is the subtle suggestion that entering the temple defiles it just as the Babylonians' or Assyrians' entering of Oholah ("tent") or Oholibah ("my tent is in her") defiled the women. Put most simply, this imagery implies that the temple is not merely a cipher for Jerusalem but the equivalent of her reproductive organs. The language in Lam 1:9-10, in particular the proximity of the terms for "defilement," "skirts," and "temple," suggests what may appear to be a stunning and somewhat unsettling notion. Given the biblical idiom that we have been tracing, however, our conclusion seems warranted. That 1:9 refers to the uncleanness of her skirts suggests two unseemly possibilities. The uncleanness may be a result of her allowing illicit entry on the one hand or, on the other, it may be the result of foreigners forced entry and resulting defilement.[5] In either case, the temple now seems to be understood as the woman who has been penetrated and defiled. Jerusalem and the temple have been raped. Should this reading seem to press the imagery and language of Lamentations, we next turn to a text that is much more explicit in associating not only women with the temple but also in associating the rape and consequent defilement of one with the other.

Judith

The book of Judith is found in what Protestants call the Apocrypha, known by Catholics as the deuterocanonical literature. Found in the LXX, or Greek translation of the Hebrew Bible, Jews do not consider the books that comprise the Apocrypha canonical. Judith's date of composition is somewhat unclear but the consensus places it in the middle to late second century B.C.E. At least 350 years later than Ezekiel and Lamentations, and outside the canon of many Christians and all Jews, one might ask why we look at Judith at all. There are several good reasons, chief among them Judith represents decades, even centuries, of the development of the theme that is the topic of this chapter. As a late representative of the temple-as-woman motif, Judith is a suggestive place to investigate the progression of this biblical motif. Moreover, one often finds in Jewish material from the late Second Temple period just this kind of elaboration on material that is the result of years of speculation and interpretation. In the end, however, the value of Judith for our investigation lies in the degree to which it illumines our understanding of the earlier forms of the temple-as-woman motif.

The focus of our attention will be chapter 9, but a brief summary of the story that precedes is necessary. The historical and geographical inaccu-

racies of the book of Judith are famous. To cite only the most glaring difficulty: Judith has Nebuchadnezzar as the king of the Assyrians rather
than the Babylonians. Despite the difficulties with the text, we can follow the main outline of the action. The Assyrians are on a military cam-
paign in the region of Israel and have successfully conquered a number of
cities in the area. Judith and the inhabitants of her hometown of Bethulia
are under siege and contemplating surrender in only a few days when
Judith announces that she has a secret plan to eliminate the threat (8:32-
34). It is important to note that the name *Bethulia* means "maiden" and
suggests that the town about to be invaded is virgin territory.

In Jdt 9, our heroine prays that her mission be successful by recalling
an event, known to any biblically literate audience, from Gen 34. In that
text, Shechem, a non-Israelite, rapes Dinah, the daughter of Jacob and
sister to his twelve sons. After the rape, Shechem comes to Jacob and his
sons and suggests that he marry Dinah and that his townspeople intermarry with Jacob and his family. Jacob's sons reply, "speaking with guile
because he had defiled [*t-m-'*] their sister Dinah" (Gen 34:13), that so
long as Shechem and his people would undergo circumcision, they were
willing to intermarry. After Shechem and his townsmen are circumcised,
Simeon and Levi, two of Dinah's brothers, slay all of the men when they
are incapacitated, take captive all of the women and children, and take
as booty all property. When Jacob learns of the preceding events, he asks
why they have acted in such a manner. Simeon and Levi respond,
"Should our sister be treated like a whore [*z-n-h*]?" The use of the familiar terms for defiling (*t-m-'*) and whore (*z-n-h*) suggests that the notions
we traced in the Prophets above had deep roots in Israelite literary tradition and, in particular, had currency in the narrative idiom of Genesis as
well.

Judith's prayer begins in 9:2 where we read, "O Lord God of my ancestor Simeon, to whom you gave a sword to take revenge on those strangers
who had torn off a virgin's clothing to defile [*miasma*] her, and exposed
her thighs to put her to shame, and polluted [*ebebēlōsan*] her womb to
disgrace her" (NRSV). Having invoked the rape of Dinah, Judith goes on
in her prayer to remind God that Shechem and his townsmen were properly punished for their misdeeds and, further, to suggest that should he
desire, he can help again (vv. 3-6).[6] Judith next announces that the arro-
gant Assyrians are ready for the attack, ignorant of the fact that God is
the "Lord of wars" (v. 7 NRSV). In verse 8, Judith says, "Break their
strength by your might, and bring down their power in your anger; for

they intend to defile [*bebēlōsai*] your sanctuary, and to pollute [*mianai*] the tabernacle where your glorious name resides" (NRSV). As the story of Judith comes to a climax, she cunningly gains entrance into the camp of the Assyrians, gains the trust of their commander, Holofernes, and eventually beheads him. On return to Bethulia, she displays Holofernes's head, and the Jews, emboldened by Judith's bravery, put the Assyrians to flight.

There are a number of significant issues that arise in the book of Judith that we shall address, but first, and obviously the most important, is the clear association between the rape of Dinah and the impending entrance into the temple by the Assyrians. Note that the author of Judith applies the same language of pollution and defilement to Dinah and the temple. Whereas Ezekiel's wife's death was a cipher for the loss of the temple, he makes no further elaboration of the association between the two. In Lamentations we saw that the text alludes to the sexual equivalence of the temple and a woman in the language of defilement and penetration, but it is with Judith that all of the dots are fully connected. In order to understand this explicit depiction of the tabernacle/temple in vaginal imagery, we need to consider several important issues.

Written around the time of the Maccabean revolt in ca. 165 B.C.E., Judith reflects many of the Jewish anxieties of the age, in particular, the anxiety of cultural and religious preservation. In this sense, the book is in step with the prophetic anxieties, but with a change. Whereas for the prophets sexual improprieties represented Israel's willful promiscuity, Judith reflects a culture that had been subservient for centuries. This anxiety over cultural interpenetration and assimilation is key to understanding Judith and the ways in which it depicts the events therein.[7] Using the story of Dinah from Gen 34 is a masterstroke because it reflects many of the same anxieties over assimilation. Note that in that story Shechem and his townsmen are circumcised, a sort of symbolic decapitation, only after he has defiled Dinah. Judith sets this travesty right buy making sure that the "head" of the Assyrians is decapitated before he and his men can pollute or defile the temple.[8] In Judith, as opposed to the prophets, Jews are understood less as perpetrators of sexual improprieties than they are victims. Yet, according to Judith, the type of illicit penetration suffered by Dinah is miraculously prevented.

How is it, then, that the temple comes to represent the corporate identity of Israel or the Jews? It is at least in part the legacy of the prophetic marriage/adultery motif. Recall that for the prophets Israel/Judah were understood as God's female partner and that Jerusalem in Jeremiah and Ezekiel was depicted by synecdoche in equally feminine imagery. It is by further refinement of the "part for whole" dynamic that the temple could be understood as woman as well. Ezekiel 24 does just this, as does Lamentations. Judith reflects the evolution of this dynamic in a new historical period. Now the temple can be understood as a woman, but rather than seeking out lovers, she must protect herself from unwanted ones. Recall that in the late prophetic idiom, especially in Ezekiel, the promiscuity of Judah was understood to defile the temple. To the degree that the temple was the innocent victim there, Judith is in keeping with such a conceptualization.

This association of the temple with the tradition of God's beloved is remarkable both in its development and for its significance. In this transition, we move from the prophetic notion that the people of Israel or Judah owe their sexual (religious) fidelity to God to a variation in which the temple represents the embodiment of God's desire. In the Prophets, in particular Jer 2 and Hos 2, the exodus and wilderness wanderings are conceived as the honeymoon in this ancient but tenuous relationship. There is a contrast between present reality and the optimistic origins of the love affair. In the temple-as-woman motif there is no looking back to better days; rather, it looks at the pain of loss and defilement. Not only is this reality drawn in vivid language and imagery, it is also remarkably present and contemporaneous to the narrators. No longer the jilted lover, God is understood to have lost his beloved, the delight of his eyes. Judith, in contrast to the history the author had to know, keeps the archetypal enemy, the Assyrians, from the penetration of the temple that Lamentations, *mutatis mutandis*, records. This type of fiction is common to a culture so traumatized by the past. For the author of Judith and its audience, the hope, even prayer, is that this penetration and defilement would never, could never, happen again.

Beyond the immediacy of the temple-as-woman motif, note the presumption that the temple, as womb, is understood to be appropriately occupied only by God. Understood as the locus of his presence, it is where he preserves his people. The temple was once understood as an inviolable guarantee of Israelite and Jewish safety (see Jer 7). The narrators now understand that whatever God's desire for his people and temple, with its destruction he has suffered the loss of his beloved. Concomitant with that loss is the loss of protection against assimilation and the degradation of identity. In the later and fuller version of this motif found in Judith, we see expressed the late Second Temple hope that God's desire and chivalry remain strong enough to protect his "bride." In reality, while the period in which Judith was likely written saw the Seleucids defile the temple, the Maccabees were able to repel them and to rededicate it. To the extent that the temple actually was defiled, Judith's account becomes even more fictional.

With Judith we have a later variation on the temple-as-woman motif and, as such, a conception that was to have powerful influence on the next two centuries. In an era when confidence in prophecy had disappeared and an unlikely victory and subsequent autonomy established, the temple became one of the foci of the theology of love. Now, the temple seems to become the embodiment of the notion of God's bride, and his continued presence witness to his continuing commitment to the relationship. This notion, of course, would face the second great challenge to the theology of love in the destruction of the Second Temple in 70 C.E. We shall take up the consequences of that tragic event in the last chapter of this study; for now we need to turn to a theological construct in the Hebrew Bible that has resonance with the temple-as-woman motif and that provides a connection to our discussion in chapter 3.

The Temple and Eden

Jon Levenson has pointed out several places in the Hebrew Bible that identify the temple with Eden.[9] He notes that Ezek 28:13-14 makes just this kind of identification and argues, "This builds, in turn, upon the conception of the temple as paradise—the world in its ideal state, the world as its creator hoped it would be."[10] Part of the identification of the temple with Eden relies on imagery of fertility. In particular, some of the psalms describe the temple in luxuriant imagery associated with gardens and often in images of fresh water flowing through an edenic landscape (Pss 92:13-16; 36:6-11).[11] Furthermore, this water is often associated with the fountain of life. Levenson points out that Ezek 47:1-12 tells of a restored temple from which waters issue forth to sustain the world and make it fertile. In particular, the temple seems to be understood as a renewed and renewing Eden.

Levenson provides these fine insights for the purpose of arguing that the image of the temple is often one of life and one that holds the promise of redemption in the Hebrew Bible. For our purposes, he could not have made a clearer case for the argument herein. The temple, understood as a woman and womb is also, in parts of the Hebrew Bible, associated with Eden and the origins of human life. As such, it represents the safe haven from which humans derive their sustenance and can trace their ultimate origins and final redemption. We shall see in the next chapter that Torah was similarly linked with Eden and, more consistently, with imagery of water and fertility. That the temple and Torah came to be understood in categories of fertility, sustenance, and redemption associated with the garden of Eden is a crucial link in tracing the theology of love in the Hebrew Bible.

Summary of the Temple, Women, and Wombs

All of the texts we have considered in this chapter presume a remarkably intimate and touching vision of the temple. In varying degrees, the temple represents the vulnerability of both God and his people. While the temple is subject to defilement and consequent alienation of God from his people, it is conceived, in ideal terms and times, as the protective womb for God and his people—an ever-present Eden, if you will. Moreover, the temple is the source of fertility of Israel/Judah and the source of life, redemption, and renewal. In a perfect world, the temple represented God's beneficent presence among his people. In the imagery of sexual intimacy, the temple provided a central means of articulating the theology of love in much of the Hebrew Bible and the Second Temple period. We next turn to another means by which God's intimacy was understood in imagery remarkably similar to that associated with the temple.

WOMEN, WELLS, WISDOM, AND TORAH

W hile the theology of love found articulation in the Second Temple period in concepts surrounding the temple, it also was conceived in notions of scripture and the Torah.[1] In fact, a text we considered in the last chapter may be an early allusion to the increasing status of Scripture, or at least the word, in the period after the destruction of the first temple. Recall that at the end of Ezekiel's sign-act, in which his wife's death represented the destruction of the temple, YHWH tells him that on the day the temple is destroyed he will again be able to speak. Whether intentional or not, the regaining of speech with the loss of the temple represents the main religious dynamic of the exilic period; the rise of Scripture (as written rather than spoken word) and the simultaneous investment in it as a locus of God's presence with his people.[2] In support of this shifting reinvestment, F. W. Dobbs-Allsopp has argued that the woman's voice of the book of Lamentations represents a "comforting" replacement for the temple.[3] This shift was not complete or fully articulated but, clearly, its early stages are witnessed in the roughly fifty years that Judah spent in exile in Babylonia.[4] That they were released by the Persians and allowed to return to the land and rebuild the temple merely slowed the transition to words and, eventually, to the Torah as the second main embodiment of the theology of love. This chapter investigates the origins of this shift and considers both the background to the notion of Scripture as God's presence as well as the ways it developed in the late Second Temple period.

In order to proceed, it is necessary to consider a few important points that have arisen so far in our study. Integral to the prophetic marriage/adultery and temple-as-woman motifs is the association of God's presence with fertility. In particular, Hos 2 was most eloquent in depicting the fruitful nature of the relationship when it went well. There is a corresponding lack of fertility when it did not. Clearly, embedded in the notion of the temple as woman, the loss of the temple triggered an equally disastrous result for hopes of continued fertility, not withstanding Ezekiel's moving vision of a renewed temple in 47:1-12. In tracing the emergence of the rise in status of scripture and its association with the theology of love, we need first to recognize that learning and wisdom came to be associated with Scripture, especially in the Second Temple period. Often, the value of learning and study of God's instruction was represented by imagery associated with water and fertility. Psalm 1 is a great place to start to elaborate on the key issues that occupy us in this chapter. Psalm 1 reads:

> Happy is the man who has not followed the counsel of the wicked,
>> or taken the path of sinners,
>> or joined the company of the insolent;
>> rather, the teaching [*torah*] of the LORD is his delight,
>> and he studies that teaching [*torah*] day and night.
> He is like a tree planted beside the streams of water,
>> which yields its fruit in season,
>> whose foliage never fades,
>> and whatever it produces thrives.
> Not so the wicked;
>> rather, they are like chaff that wind blows away.
> Therefore the wicked will not survive judgment,
>> nor will sinners, in the assembly of the righteous.
> For the LORD cherishes the way of the righteous,
>> but the way of the wicked is doomed.

Known as a Wisdom psalm, Ps 1 has much to do with the association of wisdom with Torah and both of these with water. Note that the word *torah* appears twice in the psalm. While it is not likely that *torah* refers to the proper name for Scripture in this psalm, this is precisely how the term came to be understood in the history of interpretation.[5] More important is the imagery employed here. Note that the disciplined man who studies or recites the teaching of the Lord is compared to a tree planted beside a stream of water.[6] In this imagery the tree, as representative of the wise man, flourishes and produces fruit—is fully fertile. In this analogy, the teaching (*torah*) of the Lord is associated with water, the properties of which, of course, are to sustain and support the life of the fertile tree.

In the remainder of this chapter we shall investigate the origins of the notions presumed by Ps 1 and, in turn, look to the Second Temple period to see how the theology of love came to be associated with the Torah. Moreover, we shall consider how the evolution of the imagery of fertility enriches the association of the Torah with women.

Genesis

The book of Genesis may seem an odd place to start our investigation, but certain texts therein provide essential background for understanding the developments that we shall consider in this chapter. From the first command to humans to be fertile and multiply in Gen 1:28, there is an association of creation with fertility. More important, in Gen 2–3, the second creation, or J account, the text associates the garden of Eden, perhaps the most fecund locale imaginable, with God's presence and the fertility of humans. Beginning with a world devoid of plants, rain, and humans to till the earth (Gen 2:5), a mist comes up out of the ground and waters the surface of the earth (v. 6). The source of this moisture is unclear other than that it, like man in verse 7, comes from the ground itself. In verse 7 we are told that YHWH fashions the first man out of the dust of the earth. In Gen 2:8, right after the Lord has fashioned the man, YHWH plants the garden of Eden and places the man there. The fecund images multiply in the next few verses when YHWH causes trees to sprout in the garden and when we are told of the four rivers that well up from within it to water it (vv. 9-14). Perhaps we are to envision some kind of oasis in a deserted world, but whatever the case may be, we have a stunning image of a new fertile world in which man has been placed. Indeed, Eden appears to represent the womb of humanity. This imagery continues with the creation of various animals meant to be the company of man until YHWH eventually puts man to sleep and produces the woman (vv. 15-22). All of this comes to a climax in verse 23 when the man, Adam, declares:

43

This one is the bone of my bone and flesh of my flesh
To this one is given the name woman, since from man was she
taken. (AT)

It is hard to imagine a more powerful way to stress the identity of the
first two humans. So much do their identities converge that even their
names are essentially inseparable. The English pair man/woman nicely
replicates the Hebrew pair *'ish/'ishah*. Genesis 2:24 concludes with the
famous dictum, "On account of this man leaves his father and mother and
clings to his wife that they might become one flesh" (AT). Integral to the
fertile imagery and language of Gen 2 is the culmination of all that
has happened in the reference to the consummation of the love between
man and woman. With this in mind, it is fascinating that the last verse
of chapter 2 contains the famous verbal link to the first half verse of
chapter 3:

And the two of them were <u>nude</u> (*'arummim*), the man and his wife,
but were unashamed.
Now the snake was more <u>shrewd</u> (*'arum*) than all other animals of
the field that YHWH had made. (AT)

The underlined words in the translation are of central importance in
these verses. The pair *nude* and *shrewd* comes close to implying what the
Hebrew connotes. The innocence that marks sexuality in the garden is
now in the process of change, and the use of such similar lexical items as
'arummim (*'-w-r*) and *'arum* (*'-r-m*) marks the shift to a new perspective. The word pair, with nearly identical pronunciation in Hebrew, signals the shift from the innocence in the garden to the emergence of the
guile of human sexuality and the suspect nature of sexual desire and
motive. Two issues of note arise from this verse. First is the recognition
that, to some degree, the Song of Songs represents a protracted celebration of the guileless sexuality lost when Adam and Eve are expelled from
the garden.[7] The Song resonates with this sentiment of unashamed
human sexuality and, by association, the implied fertility represented by
the garden. Secondly, the language of nakedness appears here in con-
tradistinction to the prophetic use. To the degree that the story of the garden of Eden presents the ideal of human sexuality, the prophets present
the degree to which sexuality can go wrong.

Examples of the ways that Gen 3 depicts this emergent guile can be
seen especially in 3:6 where, upon reflection, Eve recognizes that not

only would the tree provide good food, but it is beautiful and "appropriate for discernment" as well (AT).[8] Moreover, in 3:8, Adam and Eve hide when they hear God walking around the garden, and in verses 12 and 13 we see the successive deferral of blame from Adam to Eve to the snake. That Adam and Eve eat from the tree of the knowledge of good and evil is, of course, of pivotal importance in our story. It is with this knowledge that their nudity (*ʿ-w-r*) dawns on them. Given the association in 2:25 and 3:1 of *nude* and *shrewd* we are likely to understand that their self-consciousness is essentially sexual and implies the guile demonstrated the instant they hide from God and attempt to shift blame for their actions.

The garden story represents deep and long-lived reflection on human nature and, in particular, the nature of human sexuality. The story looks with envy on the time when sexual innocence prevailed.[9] Most significant is the persistent and unblinking reflection on sexuality's connection to the garden. At this level, the garden becomes a trope for the location of innocent sexuality before it becomes immersed in the quagmire of human vulnerability, scheming, and guile. But there is no simple way to read the story of the garden of Eden because it represents, in important ways, the kind of reflection that it critiques. In other words, no simple or univocal reading of the garden story does justice to its subtlety. It, like the snake, is likely too smart for its own good.[10] That is, the story seems to be aware at some level that its own reflection on sexuality is part of the original problem. There is no going back to the garden, and the story presumes this at every turn. Indeed, as we all know, the story ends with the expulsion of Adam and Eve from the garden, which is, if you like, now "a garden locked" (Song 4:12).

We have seen in Gen 1–3 two key sexual images that lay the foundation for the rest of this chapter. As suggested above, not just the imagery of the garden but also the imagery of water at its center represents its fertility. Certainly this imagery is consistent with texts we have considered above. Recall Hos 2:21-24 and the declaration of YHWH that he would espouse Israel forever. There, the imagery of rain and the fertile response of the earth is a clear sign of the connection between YHWH, water, and fertility. There is a text in the middle of the Song of Songs that also makes the connection between gardens and water that serves well to launch our consideration of wells and springs in Genesis.

We have noted that Eden's fecundity is an important part of the story of the first man and woman and the locus of their origin and apparent marriage (2:23-25). Song 4:12–5:1 frames its reference to a garden in analogously luxuriant language, as we read:

> A garden locked is my sister and bride, a fountain stopped, a spring sealed.
> Your limbs are an orchard of pomegranates filled with sweet fruit— with henna and nard. Nard and saffron,
> reeds and cinnamon with all fragrant woods,
> myrrh and aloes with all the best perfumes.

> A garden spring, a well of living water, a brook flowing out of Lebanon.
> North wind awake, south wind enter, waft over my garden, spread its perfume.
> Let my love enter his garden, and eat its sweet fruit.
> I have entered my garden, my sister, bride, have plucked my perfumed myrrh.
> I have eaten my honey and its comb, drunk my wine with milk.

> Eat lovers—drink, be intoxicated with love.

This truly beautiful poetry celebrates the affection of its two lovers in remarkably vivid imagery. In particular, we need to focus on the language used here. This rich and fecund locus of human love is much like the garden of Eden.[11] Again, in many respects this text celebrates the innocence of love that seems unrecoverable after the events in Eden.[12] More significant is that the first "couple" in Genesis is to be as fertile as the garden they inhabit. Indeed, it is only through the fertility of that first couple that God is able to maintain his creation and his relation therewith. In this sense, human and divine fertility are integrally related. Hosea's message, especially in chapter 2, depends heavily on this fundamental insight. Human love and sexuality in Eden are integral to the larger creative act of God and central to the continuation thereof. The garden, then, becomes a metaphor that makes human and divine fertility inseparable.

But understanding the garden as metaphor has a secondary aspect. Human sexuality metaphorically replicates the fertility of God and provides the progeny through which God maintains his association with creation. In this way, human sexuality should be understood as the vehicle by which God relates to humans. Procreation enacts re-creation. All of this suggests that the language of the garden in Genesis is profitably understood in the larger frame of ancient Israelite idiom that understands the love of humans as essentially inseparable from the love of God.

The prophetic conflation of human intercourse with metaphorical adultery understood as apostasy becomes much clearer once we consider the other key element that frames our discussion. In particular, we need to turn to a consideration of the use of the language of springs and wells (*'-y-n* and *b-'-r*) in Genesis. Through this investigation we will see that the Hebrew Bible's use of metaphor is highly nuanced. The language of springs/wells and garden is metaphorical for both human relations and relations between humans and God. Because both human and divine relations are dependent on the same metaphorical language, it is hard to make absolute distinctions between them. In fact, in Genesis, this language makes inseparable the notion of human relations and human relations with God. This conceptual "DNA" goes far in explaining why early interpreters saw in the Song of Songs an account of God's abiding affection for his people.

A Spring Sealed

Significantly, the two halves of Song of Songs 4:12–5:1 begin with the language of springs or wells. Note that after referring to his lover as a "spring sealed" in verse 12, the man again refers to his lover in similar language in verse 15 but with important changes. Here the woman is referred to as a "garden spring" and as a "well of living waters." The multiple levels at which this can be understood are fascinating, but of greatest interest is the reinforced notion of the woman as the source of life. In order to understand more fully the well imagery in Song of Songs, the following discussion considers the language of wells and springs in Genesis as a means to understand the significance of well imagery in this and other parts of the Hebrew Bible.

The image of wells appears in Genesis and Exodus stories containing what Robert Alter has called the "betrothal type scene."[13] Alter deals with three texts of special interest for our purposes: Gen 24:10-61; 29:1-20; and Exod 2:15b-21. One element of this type scene particularly important for the current discussion is that each betrothal begins at the scene of a well. In Gen 24 it is Abraham's servant, sent to find a mate for Isaac, who meets Rebekah at a spring (*'-y-n* in vv. 13, 16, 29, 42, 43, 45) and a well (*b-'-r* in v. 29). In Gen 29 Jacob meets Rachel for the fist time at a "well of the field" (*b-'-r* three times in v. 2, two times in v. 3, and once each in vv. 8 and 10, AT). Finally, Moses meets his wife, Zipporah, and her sisters at a well in Exod 2 (*b-ʾ-r* in v. 15b).

The alternation between the imagery of springs and wells signals that both sources of water represent fertility, and this connection is significant to our text in Song 4:15 where spring and well are placed in apposition, functioning essentially as synonyms. Alter's type scene has pointed out a very useful way of understanding these events in the patriarchal narrative. In fact, Alter also calls attention to the connection between fertility and the language of springs and wells central to our discussion. He notes that the "well . . . is obviously a symbol of fertility and, in all likelihood, also a female symbol."[14] In this instance, Alter could have been bolder. It seems indubitable that the imagery of springs/wells in these stories represent fertility, women, and, indeed, their wombs.

With the preceding in mind, it is necessary to consider in detail a number of texts in Genesis that help give a fuller sense of this idiomatic use of the imagery of wells and springs. We begin with a brief consideration of the texts identified by Alter and then turn to a number of other texts that seem to presuppose similar understanding of this literary idiom. The longest of the betrothal type scenes requires the least of our time. In this story Abraham's servant travels to Aram-naharaim to find a wife for Isaac (Gen 24). As expected, he meets Rebekah at a spring near the city of Nahor. Upon meeting, Rebekah draws water from the spring and gives not only Abraham's servant a drink, but also all ten of his camels. While this imagery suggests the fertility that is represented by Rebekah, the spring is less obviously a cipher for her future role as mother of Isaac's children. In the episode of Jacob's meeting with Rachel, however, the role of the source of water as cipher for her is clearer.

In Gen 29:1-20 we read of the first time Jacob encounters Rachel. In verses 1-3 we learn that in the land where he has arrived there is a well and that, when the locals wish to water their sheep, they must roll a stone away from the mouth of the well. In verses 10-11, when Jacob meets Rachel, he rolls the stone away from the well, waters her flock, and then kisses her. The language in verses 10b-11a is of interest. Here we read:

> Jacob rolled the stone away from the mouth of the well and <u>watered</u> the flock of Laban his uncle, then Jacob <u>kissed</u> Rachel. (AT)

The image of the stone that blocks the well evokes nicely the fact that Rachel is said to be barren (29:31) and Jacob's rolling of the stone away further brings to mind the time when her womb is opened by God (30:22).[15]

Further, it is tempting to see in the language of these verses another hint at the way the well is equated with Rachel. Note that Jacob removes the stone from the mouth of the well to water (*sh-q-h*) the flock, and he then kisses (*n-sh-q*) Rachel. In the Hebrew, because each of the roots has a weak consonant, the consonants of the two verbs are written identically as *wyshq*. Perhaps we make too much of the recurrence of the consonants for the words "to water" and "to kiss," but even if the language here is coincidental, it is highly suggestive of the association of Rachel with the well, and thus her role as the source of Jacob's most crucial progeny. It takes little imagination to see that this well represents not only fertility but also Rachel's womb. Finally, we shall see that the history of interpretation focused on these two roots as they appear in Song 1 and associated them as well.

The last of Alter's betrothal type scenes that we need to consider is found in Exod 2. While this story is found outside of Genesis, it is of great help in tracing the significance of the imagery of wells and springs in the narrative idiom. In Exod 2:15b-22 Moses, fleeing Egypt for the first time, enters Midian and sits by a well. When the daughters of the priest of Midian come to water their sheep, local shepherds try to drive them away. Seeing this, Moses defends the girls and waters their flock. He subsequently is invited to the priest's house where Moses eventually marries Zipporah, who will bear his children.

Having considered the category of betrothal type scene, what can we deduce about the use of the imagery of springs/wells in Genesis and Exodus? First, it is hard to dispute the notion that springs and wells represent fertility. On the one hand they represent the fertility of the land, and on the other, the fertility of the people of God. As a result, the spring represents a cipher for the woman in each scene, a point made most clearly with the imagery of Jacob removing the stone, which seals the spring, that so nicely resonates with the eventual opening of Rachel's womb and subsequent conception of Joseph and Benjamin. We turn next to a number of texts in Genesis that rely on this same metaphor.

Under consideration are several texts that resonate with the betrothal type scene but represent significant variations on that form. The first two texts from Gen 16 and 38 appear to have some association with the meeting of the patriarch and his mate at a spring or well, although in much less explicit terms than the three texts considered above. In the final set of texts we shall consider, the issue of betrothal is absent, but the metaphor of "a woman as well" is central.

We begin with a passage in Gen 16 that, on first glance, may seem unrelated to our discussion but, on reflection, likely relates to it in subtle ways. Genesis 16 tells the story of Sarah's ploy to solve her barrenness by having Abraham engender children with Hagar. Sarah makes Hagar's life miserable once she realizes that Hagar has conceived, so the maidservant runs away. Of interest is Gen 16:7 where an angel of the Lord finds Hagar at "a spring [ʿ-y-n] in the wilderness, the spring [ʿ-y-n] on the way to Shur" (AT). The message that the angel of God has for Hagar is to go back and submit to Sarah's treatment. The news is not all bad, however, since the angel proceeds to make promises that are quite reminiscent of those given to Abraham (12:2, 13:15, 15:5, and so on). Interestingly, the closeness of these promises to those given Abraham suggests that Ishmael might be the promised son. As the narrative continues, however, it becomes clear that this is not the case (Gen 17:20-21). More importantly, Hagar, right after we are told that she has conceived and just before she receives the promises for her son, is found next to a spring. This spring represents an analogue to her fertility, especially in contrast to Sarah's barrenness. Hagar's association with a water source is evidenced next in in Gen 21, considered a second version of the story in chapter 16, where she and Ishmael wander in the wilderness until God saves them by pointing out a well (b-ʾ-r) of water. Therefore, the stories of Ishmael's birth and subsequent salvation both are located at this symbol of fertility. Genesis 16 makes most explicit the association of Hagar with the well as a symbol of her fertility, but both stories seem to be aware of the role springs and wells play in the survival of the people of Abraham. While Hagar is not the wife through whom Abraham's promises will devolve, she is depicted in ways very similar to the betrothal type scene, yet with substantial alterations. These alterations likely signal both the variability of the motif and the fact that Hagar does not have the same status in the Israelite lineage that Rebekah, Rachel, and Zipporah share.

Another text that seems to rely on resonance with the betrothal type scene while also diverging significantly from it is Gen 38. Judah, having sent Tamar away apparently to preserve his only remaining son, inadvertently propositions her on his way to Timnah. Genesis 38:14 says that Tamar was sitting at the "entrance to Enaim [ʿynym]" when Judah encountered and then propositioned her. This Hebrew phrase has always given interpreters difficulty but, in view of the persistent association of the mothers of Genesis with wells and springs, it is possible that we should understand the phrase to mean "at the opening of the two springs." According to this reading, the text signals that this is the woman with whom Judah will have his progeny. Indeed, it is the birth of Perez to Tamar and Judah that maintains the lineage of King David according to Ruth 4:18-21. Perhaps we are to take the dual form "two wells" to signal the twins that will be conceived in the ensuing liaison. What seems certain, however, is that the association of the patriarch's mate with a spring, and all the associated resonances, is likely not coincidence.

Genesis 16 and 38 suggest the variability with which the metaphor of a woman as a spring/well could be employed, though the use of the word "employed" is perhaps too loaded. It is unlikely that this metaphor is manipulated in any purposeful way, but it is more likely that the traditionary process, over multiple years and through multiple mouths and hands, slowly forms the stories based on emergent notions of cultural literacy and competence. Significantly, the variations provide differing insight into the value of the language of springs and wells and their association with women.

We next turn to a set of texts that is less concerned with the issue of betrothal but still relies heavily on the metaphor of a woman as a spring. The first text is Gen 20. This is the story of Abraham's sojourn in Gerar during which Sarah is taken into King Abimelech's household. This represents the second of what are known as the "endangered ancestress" episodes.[16] There are two elements of particular interest in this text, both of which are found in the last three verses. After returning Sarah to Abraham untouched (vv. 4, 6), Abimelech says to her:

> To Sarah he [Abimelech] said, "Look, I have given a thousand pieces of silver to your brother, let this be a 'covering of the two eyes (springs)' for all who are with you and with all a vindication." Abraham prayed and God healed Abimelech, his wives, and his slave girls and they bore children; for YHWH had sealed tight every womb in Abimelech's house on account of Sarah wife of Abraham. (AT)

The first element we must consider is the notice that YHWH had sealed tight the wombs of all the women of Abimelech's house. The language of verse 18 suggests that the closing of the wombs was in some way an appropriate response to Abimelech taking Sarah into his household. We are likely to understand that Sarah's womb was also "sealed" while there. If this is the case, it is a redundant element in the story since we have known of Sarah's barrenness since Gen 11:30, and we are told that Abimelech never approached her while she was in his house.

Nevertheless, the fact that YHWH opens the wombs after this episode may suggest why it is that in the very next chapter, only two verses later, Sarah finally conceives Isaac. Possibly we are to understand that Sarah's womb was opened at the same time, but more important is the notion that the threat to Abraham and Sarah is perceived to be the threat to their progeny. Hence the text records the punishment meted out to Abimelech in kind.

The second element of note in the passage above is the term Abimelech uses in verse 16 to describe the significance of the silver given to Abraham. Abimelech says that it will serve as a covering of the eyes/springs (*'ynym*) for her. This phrase makes the interpretation of verse 16 difficult. Many take it to be in parallelism with the last phrase in the verse and therefore understand it to say, "Let this serve as a clearing" before all. Obscurities like this are difficult to resolve, but it is noteworthy that this phrase represents something of a reversal of the imagery in Gen 38:14, a passage we have read as "the opening of the two springs." What could be the import of using this phrase, especially in light of the metaphor of a woman as a spring found throughout Genesis? If we read the phrase as it is normally understood, "a covering of the two eyes," we may be meant to understand it as a reference to Sarah's modesty and her status as a married woman. If, however, we read the phrase to mean, "a covering of the two springs," there are several possibilities. First, we might understand it to mean that Abimelech is subtly suggesting that he hopes Sarah's womb (as a spring) remains "covered" like the wombs of the women of his household. This is a possibility since Abimelech apparently does not know that Sarah was barren prior to her arrival in his household. According to this reading, the phrase "covering of the two eyes/springs" may act as a double entendre meaning both vindication and barrenness. This reading must remain speculative since the phrase is so obscure, but there is another feature of chapter 20 that lends credence to our reading of "covering of the springs" and continues to help fill in our understanding of the metaphor of a woman as a spring.

We begin by noting that Gen 21:22 is a logical continuation of the events narrated in chapter 20. Essentially, Gen 21:1-21 represent an interruption in the narrative of Abraham's dealings with Abimelech. Invariably, there are good reasons for such narrative interruptions, and it is not my purpose to suggest that the narrative as we have it does not make sense. Indeed, there is good narrative logic to have the birth of Isaac and the departure of Hagar and Ishmael where they are. I simply wish to point out the continuity between the end of chapter 20 and 21:22. This continuity includes more than just the continuation of Abraham's dealing with Abimelech. In fact, the language of 21:25 is quite familiar and serves to support the contention that we should read it with chapter 20. In 21:25 Abraham reproaches Abimelech for having seized his well (*b-ʾ-r*) of water. The result of the ensuing narrative is that Abraham and Abimelech swear an oath by which Abimelech acknowledges that the well, to be known as Beer-sheba, belongs to Abraham. Following the events of chapter 20, it is hard to miss the significance of Abraham's complaint that Abimelech has taken his "well." The juxtaposition of these texts is as close as our texts come to making explicit the association of women and wells in our narratives. In addition to the association of the well with Sarah, there is another significant element related to wells and fertility embedded in our text. According to Gen 21:30-31, the name of the well, Beer-sheba (*beʾer shavaʿ*), has a double etymology, with *shava* carrying both the meaning "oath" and "seven." Beer-sheba, therefore, means both "the well of oath" and "the well of seven." The significance of the reference to "oath" is clear, since Abraham and Abimelech swear an oath that the well belongs to Abraham. The association with seven comes from Abraham giving Abimelech seven ewes and saying, "You are to accept these seven ewes from me as proof that I dug this well." As we have seen in other passages, sheep and wells are paired in the stories of patriarchs meeting their wives at wells. The association of the well of Beer-sheba with sheep connects this passage to the betrothal scenes. This all suggests that the cultural and literary competence that informs these texts strongly links women, wells, and sheep—all symbols of fertility.[17] There is a final text we need to consider that helps at once to reinforce a number of divergent parts of our argument thus far.

Events narrated in Gen 26 confirm our suggestion that 21:22 is profitably read following chapter 20 and supports our double reading of 20:16. Genesis 26:1-16 represents the third of the famous endangered-ancestress episodes: this one about Isaac and Rebekah at Abimelech's court. The presence of Gen 26:17-22 immediately following the "endangered ancestress" episode has much in common with 21:22-34. Most important is the notice that Isaac departs from Abimelech and digs the wells of Abraham that the Philistines had stopped up after Abraham's death (vv. 17-18). The juxtaposition of the "endangered ancestress" with the "dispute over wells" in Gen 26 supports the notion that the two elements are profitably read in sequence in Gen 20 and 21, where Abraham departs from Abimelech only to later fall into dispute over the wells Abimelech had seized. This juxtaposition in chapter 26 lends support to the claim that the fertility metaphor of a woman as a spring/well is operative in each case, as is the metaphor of the fertility of Israel. In particular, the fact that the "dispute over the well" topos follows the endangered-ancestress episode suggests that the former is an abstract and symbolic enactment of the events in the latter. The evidence suggests that the juxtaposition of these two literary elements was because of the cultural and literary competence of the tradents of our stories. The two stories were perceived to belong next to each other, likely because each, in its own way, attempts to depict the same threat to the longevity of Israel. Placing the stories together implies that the survival of Israel hangs in the balance: should Israel lose its springs or wells, the promises of God become irrelevant. This all makes perfect sense when one thinks back to the promises to Abraham and the other patriarchs. The promise is for land and progeny, both of which must continue to be productive if Israel is to survive (Gen 12:1-3; 13:15, and so on).

Genesis 26 makes an important addition to the "dispute over wells" that makes it especially significant for this study. Note that Abraham's complaint in chapter 21 was that Abimelech had seized his well. In that instance, the seizure of the well appears to be the narrative analogue to the taking of Sarah into his household. In chapter 26, the complaint is that Abimelech has stopped up the wells that Abraham had dug. The implication is that a stopped-up well is as much a threat to Israel as one that is no longer under their control. The image of a stopped-up well finds strange resonance with Abimelech's word to Sarah in 20:16 where he tells her that the money given to Abraham will be a "covering of the 'eyes/springs' for all around," a phrase we suggested can be read as a double entendre that sounded like "let this be a vindication" while also connoting "may your womb remain stopped up." Though the phrase's interpretation remains difficult because of its obscurity, its resonance with the events in Gen 26:17-22 is remarkable. Moreover, in context, should we understand Abimelech's words to refer to Sarah's womb/spring, they are ironically reversed when only a few verses later we learn that Sarah has conceived and that, like the women of Abimelech's court, her womb has been opened.

Summary of Gardens, Springs, and Wells in Genesis

From our discussion of the imagery of springs and wells in Genesis, a number of things appear to be relatively sure. It is difficult to deny the persistent association of women, and especially their wombs, with springs and wells. In the betrothal type scene, the imagery represents fertility in general, and the promise of the fertility of the woman in question specifically. We have also seen that the betrothal type scene likely lies behind the events depicted in Gen 16 and 38. At the very least, these two chapters support the notion that the spring imagery is consistently employed in stories about women's sexual liaisons and subsequent conception. The two endangered-ancestress episodes, followed as they are by the "dispute over the well," make even more explicit the association of springs and wells with the women of Genesis. More significantly, these stories convey the threat to the divine promises posed by the taking of both women and the springs/wells that represent them.

Having established the prominence and centrality of the imagery of wells and springs and their association with women, we next turn to other texts in the Hebrew Bible that seem to presume similar associations. It is in the evolution of this imagery and the variations upon it that we begin to trace the emergence of the association of women, wells, and Torah.

Proverbs 5

We turn to Proverbs for an example of how Wisdom literature came to understand the association of women and wells. In Prov 5:15-18 a young man is instructed to avoid a foreign woman in the following way:

> Drink the water of your own cistern, the fresh water of your well [*b-ʾ-r*].
> Your springs [*ʿ-y-n*] will flow outward, streams of water in the square.
> Let them alone be yours, not some foreign woman.
> Blessed be your fountain, may you rejoice in the wife of your youth.
> (AT)

Here, the young man's wife is referred to as a cistern, well, spring, stream, and fountain.[18] Of considerable import is that the discussion of the danger of the foreign woman comes in the part of Proverbs that urges the young man to listen to his father and to dedicate himself to Wisdom. Wisdom (*kh-k-m*) is a feminine noun and represents the woman to whom the young man ought to be loyal and even married. In this sense, Wisdom as the woman represented by the various sources of water is the means by which the young man maintains his relationship to God (cf. Prov 2:1-6, and so on). Instructive are Prov 3:19 and 8:22 where Wisdom is either the means of creation or the first thing created. These verses apparently rely on the association of Wisdom/woman/water and may presume that the water at the origin of creation is the female principle called Wisdom. Clearly, Proverb's reliance on this imagery of woman as well, which serves as the crucial link to God's fullness, has a tradition behind it. In fact, part of that tradition is found in the stories of Genesis. To understand fully the use of the imagery of springs and wells in Genesis requires recognizing that Proverbs, whatever its temporal relation to Genesis, shares with it very similar religio-literary competence and conventions.[19]

The careful reader may have noticed another significant element of Prov 5:15-18. A foreign woman is understood to be a threat to the boy and his dedication to Wisdom. In the book of Proverbs, Wisdom is anthropomorphic and, at times, seems to take on divine aspects. This is likely because Wisdom, as a result of the study of both the father's and God's teachings (cf. Ps 1), was understood to have divine origins. If we are to understand Wisdom as a type of female divine counterpart to God, and there is good reason to do so, then we have in Prov 5 a remarkable reversal of the prophetic marriage/adultery motif. In the latter, recall that Israel is understood as the wife of God, and her infidelity (apostasy) is depicted as whoring and promiscuity. Here in Proverbs, the genders have reversed; now Israel, represented by the young man, is instructed to maintain fidelity to his wife, Wisdom. While not explicit, we saw something of the same reversal in Nahum and the surprising application of the nakedness-exposed motif to Nineveh.

We have seen the predominance of the association of women with wells in the narrative idiom, in particular how it is employed in Genesis. Furthermore, we see that, likely because the Hebrew term for Wisdom (*khokhmah*) is feminine, Wisdom is associated with women and wells. This association brings to notions of Wisdom the ideas of fertility and sustenance as well. The final stage through which Torah comes to be part of this constellation of imagery associated with the theology of love is complex but worth exploring.

We mentioned Prov 8:22 above in our discussion of Prov 5, but the former deserves more extended discussion. Proverbs 8:22-23 record the words of Wisdom herself. It reads:

> The LORD created me at the beginning of His course
> As the first of His works of old.
> In the distant past I was fashioned,
> At the beginning, at the origin of earth.

Here, Wisdom makes a remarkable claim; she was the first of all of YHWH's creation. Readers and early interpreters of this verse strove to understand precisely what it means. In doing so, as always, they paid close attention to the language of the verse. Note that in 8:22 she claims that she was created (*q-n-h*) at the "beginning" of YHWH's course.[20] The Hebrew used in this instance is from the root *r-'-sh* and is the identical term used as the first word of Genesis.[21] Early interpreters saw in this coincidence a hint that Gen 1:1, in its first word, signaled the presence of Wisdom at creation.[22] One can understand this reading given the association of Wisdom with water, wells, and fertility. As our discussion of Sirach, below, will reveal, Wisdom's presence at creation explained many things for the ancient reader, including the rich and fecund nature of the world described. When they read of the fertility of the first pair of humans and their home, Eden, they likely understood that Wisdom was present. While we cannot know for sure, the assumption that Wisdom was there from the beginning of creation may have suggested an answer to a vexing problem in Gen 1:26 as well. To whom was God talking in Gen 1:26 when he said: "Let us make . . ."? By the late third or early second centuries B.C.E., Jewish tradition had come to presume that Wisdom was present at creation. Proof of this assertion is found in Sir 24, to which we now must turn.

Sirach 24

Likely written around 180 B.C.E., the book represents a relatively late version of the great Jewish Wisdom literature of the type we see in Proverbs. In fact, Sir 24 can be read as an extended commentary and elaboration of Prov 8:22–9:12.[23] In Sir 24:3 we read that Wisdom praises herself:

"I came forth from the mouth of
   the Most High,
and covered the earth like a mist." (NRSV)

In light of this verse, the tradition of understanding Wisdom, including all its associations with water and fertility, makes better sense. Sirach, aware that in Prov 8:22 Wisdom claims to have been created first, and aware that God creates everything in Gen 1 by word, assumes that Wisdom came from God's very own mouth. In fact, in Wisdom of Solomon 9:1-2 (a text included in the Apocrypha and dated to the late first century B.C.E.), word and Wisdom are synonymous and are the means by which God created the world. Note, too, that God's word, Wisdom, came out like a mist (cf. Gen 2:6) that covered the world. Sirach's reading of Prov 8 is at one and the same time creative and imaginative yet in keeping with the assumptions of its original authors. One can scarcely miss the resonance of this imagery with later interpretive traditions that see in the kisses of the Song's second verse God's giving of his Torah/ word. Sirach 24 continues to elaborate on what he sees as the significance of Wisdom's origins:

"Then the Creator of all things
   gave me a commandment,
   and the one who created me assigned a place for my tent.
And he said, 'Make your dwelling in Jacob,
and in Israel receive your inheritance.'
From eternity, in the beginning,
   he created me,
   and for eternity I shall not cease to exist.
In the holy tabernacle I ministered before him,
   and so I was established in Zion.
In the beloved city likewise he gave me a resting place,
   and in Jerusalem was my dominion.
So I took root in an honored people,
   in the portion of the LORD, who is their inheritance."
(vv. 8-12 RSV)

One can see in Sirach's words the elaboration and expansion of the meaning of Prov 8. Note that in Sir 24:8 we are to understand Wisdom's tent to be associated with the tabernacle. This becomes explicit in verse

10. Wisdom claims that her role was to minister to YHWH in the tabernacle and that she apparently continued the role in the temple built on Zion. Verse 9 is especially important for our consideration; here Wisdom claims that she was created from eternity for eternity. We are to understand that Wisdom was preexistent before creation and created to never fade.

In the next section of Sir 24:13-17, Wisdom refers to herself in language that is remarkably resonant with parts of the Song of Songs. In verse 13 she says, "I grew tall like a cedar in Lebanon, / and like a cypress on the heights of Hermon" (NRSV). She goes on to say, "Like cassia and camel's thorn I gave forth the aroma of spices, / and like choice myrrh I spread a pleasant odor, / like galbanum, onycha, and stacte, / and like the fragrance of frankincense in the Tabernacle" (v. 15 RSV). She finishes this flourish in verse 17 with, "Like a vine I caused loveliness to bud, and my blossoms became glorious and abundant fruit" (RSV). In this stunning language, Wisdom describes her comeliness in ways that are hard to resist. Whether Sirach knew the Song of Songs is hard to know, but he clearly understands Wisdom to be as seductive as the woman of the Song. More to the point, like the teaching of YHWH in Ps 1, Wisdom is associated with rich abundance and fertility. Of central significance for the theology of love in the late Second Temple period, Wisdom, as God's word, is so closely associated with the temple as well in verse 15. We see in Sirach the coalescence of the imagery of fertility, women, wells, the Word, and the tabernacle/temple.

Sirach 24:19 reads, "Come to me, you who desire me, / and eat your fill of my fruits" (NRSV). The benefits of Wisdom's fertility and fecund nature become evident in this verse; they are for all who desire her. The language and imagery here are fascinatingly resonant with Song of Songs 4:16 where we read, "Let my beloved come to his garden and enjoy its luscious fruits." In fact, the entire preceding section of Sirach, verses 13-19, reads like an elaboration and theological explanation of Song 4:12-16 as much, if not more, than a variation on Prov 8.[24] We cannot know for sure, but it seems that in this section of chapter 24, Sirach has transposed Wisdom onto Song 4:12-16 or, perhaps more likely, presumes that the Song of Songs is Wisdom literature. Whether or not this is the case, clearly Sirach's description of Wisdom is every bit as sensuous as the Song of Songs. Furthermore, it is easy to see that in Sirach's eyes, and likely in those of his contemporaries, the Song of Songs had come to be understood as Wisdom literature, a classification that remains to this day.

Moreover, so understood, the Song of Songs could be (and was) interpreted as one more example of the rich and long tradition of the theology of love.

Following the description of Wisdom in all its luxuriance and nubility, in 24:23 Sirach reveals Wisdom's true identity, "All this is the book of the covenant of the Most High God, / the law that Moses commanded us / as an inheritance for the congregations of Jacob" (NRSV). So here we have it. Sirach identifies Wisdom, with all its fertile associations, including a place in the tabernacle and temple, with Torah. To solidify its prestige and antiquity, he next likens the Torah with the great rivers of the known world: the Pishon, Tigris, Euphrates, Jordan, and Gihon. That all but the Jordan are mentioned in Gen 3:11-14 is hardly coincidence. For Sirach and his audience, Torah is the waters that issue from Eden, the source of and sustenance for all life.[25]

There is one last text relating to the traditions found in Prov 8 and Sir 24 that will help us understand the evolution of the theology of love in early interpretation to which we turn in part 2 of this work. We mentioned above that Wis 9:1-2 understands Wisdom to be synonymous with word in describing its role in creation. In Wis 8–9 we have a description of Solomon's seeming infatuation with Wisdom and, in places, what appears to be a late first-century B.C.E. rumination on the traditions we have been tracing. Of special interest is Wis 10:1–11:4 where we are told of seven historical situations in which Wisdom displayed her saving power. By the late first century B.C.E. we have all the elements that inform early interpretation of the Song. Wisdom, associated with Torah and God's word, takes center stage in the history of God's redemption of his people. As we shall see in the interpretive traditions below, the Song, apparently understood as Wisdom literature and closely associated with God's word as Torah, was understood equally to be about the saving grace of God in his peoples' history.

Summary of the Theology of Love in the Hebrew Bible

Having traced the varied traditions of the theology of love in the Hebrew Bible, it is time to summarize our findings and consider the ways it informed early interpreters of the Song of Songs. Of most significance, and perhaps most obviously, the theology of love found its two primary avenues of expression in the Second Temple period in conceptions of temple and Torah. The centrality of these two cultural institutions for the theology of love can be traced in the evolution of the marriage/adultery motif of the prophets. The prophetic anxiety over apostasy, understood as adultery, implies, from Hosea to Ezekiel, the concern over penetration and defilement. The graphic nature of the language and imagery suggests the fear that Israel or Judah, as a woman, either has been or will be defiled by illicit liaisons with her lovers.

As we have seen, while the prophetic tradition seemed to presume a linkage between the defilement of Israel/Judah with defiling the land and temple, the texts we considered in chapter 2 of this study make the connection explicit. The temple, understood as a woman, is subject to the same anxieties expressed about Israel and Judah as a whole. In this sense, the welfare of the temple was deeply connected to the welfare of the people. While this connection has subtle conceptual aspects, one must not ignore that, in a very real way, the fate of the temple and Jerusalem was the same as for the people. Furthermore, as a representative of the people, the temple was understood to be God's and his alone.[26] Here, God could sustain, support, and make fruitful his people. In the same way that God's people might be violated, so could God's temple. As suggested above, the shift that takes place in Second Temple literature is that the violation was no longer understood to be voluntary but rather the result of rape. Given the history of the Jews before and during the Second Temple period, one can easily imagine this shift from a confidence in being able to control one's destiny to the resignation that such control was a fantasy reserved for the past.

In a similar if different progression, we have seen that the Torah came to be understood as a second main support for the theology of love in the Second Temple period. This should come as no surprise. Jon Levenson has argued convincingly that Sinai, the mountain that gave Israel the Torah, and Zion, the temple mount, were transmutable in the religious conceptual world of ancient Israel.[27] Both mountains were the locus of God's presence—one in the distant past when Israel first met its God and the other in the present as God's residence. That the Torah, by association with Wisdom, could be understood as a woman further reinforced the ancient assumptions about God's connection to Israel. From the very beginning in Genesis, the presence of God was associated with water and the world's fecund response to it. In many ways, the garden of Eden serves as the female counterpart to God's fertility in Gen 1–3. Hosea and the prophetic tradition shared the notion that God's presence was, at least in part, evident from the fertility of the land. It is no surprise that later tradition, in particular the Wisdom material, came to understand Wisdom, in its associations with water and women, as a means of sustaining God's people.

That temple and Torah find their central place in the theology of love does not imply that the course of their respective evolutions was identical. Clearly, the notions that came to encircle the Torah have weaker connections to the prophetic tradition than those associated with the temple; however, recall the prophetic nostalgia for the honeymoon after the exodus and its association with Sinai and the giving of the Torah. Still, a natural distinction exists between Torah and temple. While much of Second Temple Judaism remained cautiously optimistic that the temple might remain sacrosanct, the book of Judith, as a product of the Maccabean period, testifies to the fear that it might not. No such anxiety appeared in our discussion of the development of Torah. In a special way, because it could be treasured in the hearts and memory of Jews, it could remain inviolable. In the tragic history that awaited the Jews at the beginning of the Common Era, the Torah, in addition to being mobile (much like the tabernacle had once been), had this distinct advantage over the temple. In the years following the destruction of the second temple in 70 C.E., we witness a redoubled effort to invest in the Torah as the primary remaining vestige of the tradition of God's devotion to his people.

While all this remains true, in part 2 of this study we turn to early Jewish and Christian tradition in which we see that temple, as much as Torah, remained central to their theology of love. For early interpreters, the Song of Songs came to represent the most explicit and finest example from all of Scripture of God's present devotion. We noted above that, while temple and Torah absorb something of each other's mythos, much of the Hebrew Bible conceives of Sinai as the former conduit of God's word while the temple and Zion are understood to represent his current presence. For interpreters, however, the Song, conflated with Torah, provided evidence that the theology of love was most viable through the written word, while the temple took on aspects of promises yet to be kept. It remains, then, to consider the ways in which temple and Torah continued to compose the heart of the theology of love even in the absence of the former.

PART TWO

The Theology of Love
in Early Interpretation
of the Song of Songs

I am my beloved's,
And his desire is for me.
—Song of Songs 7:11

INTRODUCTION TO EARLY INTERPRETATION

We saw in part 1 variations on the theology of love articulated in the Hebrew Bible. In part 2 we investigate early interpreters who saw in the Song of Songs the highest expression of this theology. The quote from Song 7:11 on the previous page indicates the pathos of such a vision. The hope expressed in this perspective is that God's desire would continue to be for his people.

We shall see that in both Jewish and Christian tradition, the history of the interpretation of the Song is dependent on the earliest stages of its reception. The history of the interpretation of the Song, as noted in the introduction, is one that consistently, and nearly always, saw in the Song an account of God's love for his people and associated it with the central act of redemption and renewal in their history. This is likely in large measure because of traditions like the one we discussed in Sir 24. God's presence was understood to be available through Torah, associated with Wisdom and her attendant feminine qualities, including, especially, her role in creation. The identification of Wisdom's role in the history of God's deliverance in Wis 10:1–11:4 suggested to early interpreters that the Song might too be related to that history. Indeed, the Song was heard as the refrain to the great love song that is Scripture. It was understood to serve a role common to many of the songs in the Hebrew Bible. It represented to early interpreters a condensed and highly moving account of God's history with his people.

Given the absolutely immense amount of material from the history of the interpretation of the Song, it is the goal herein to provide only a sample of what is available. In particular, we concentrate on the material preserved in the Targum (Aramaic translation) to the Song and Midrash

Rabbah among Jewish sources and on Origen among the Christian material and restrict our focus to the first four verses of Song 1. While this may seem an unreasonably narrow choice of material to cover, those familiar with the history of interpretation of the Song will realize that it is not only sufficient but even more than enough material to gain a sense of the interpreters' perspectives. Moreover, this material is representative of the ways the Song was treated in each of these sources as well as typical of the ways each of these two religious traditions came to understand the Song. The goal herein is to grapple with the interpretive material in order to expose the methods and logic of their treatment of the Song. We see in the history of early interpretation a remarkable literary competence that hears in the slightest detail echoes of the biblical tradition. It is in this larger, biblical context that the Song takes on its most vivid theological hues.

Early Jewish Interpretation

The choice of materials from early Jewish interpretation is complicated by the nature of the sources. We concentrate on the Targum and on the midrashic collection known as *Song of Songs Rabbah*. The dates of these texts are difficult to pin down with certainty. Generally, most accept that whatever date is ascribed to these two sources, each contains material that is certainly from very early in the interpretive life of the Song. To the degree one can trust the citations in these two works, it is clear that many of the interpreters cited are from the first and second centuries C.E. More important is the degree to which this material is representative of the earliest stages of Jewish interpretation. Moreover, the material contained in these works is sufficient to help define the hermeneutic focus of the early interpreters. Finally, it is from these sources that we can trace the trajectory of the history of Jewish interpretation of the Song and its formulation of the theology of love.

A last word on these two Jewish sources is in order. While we have collections known to us as the Targum and *Song of Songs Rabbah*, they, in many places, reproduce the same or similar interpretations. In other words, while the literary works are distinct, their content is not always. That the *Song of Songs Rabbah* is labeled midrash should not be taken to suggest that the Targum does not also contain midrashic interpretation. It is the nature of early Jewish interpretation that multiple sources know of similar or identical traditions.

THE TARGUM TO SONG
OF SONGS 1:1-4

The date of the Targum of the Song is unclear. Usually considered to have come into something like its present written form around the seventh to eighth century, the Targum is really an expansive commentary on the Song rather than a straightforward translation.[1] Like the other Targumim (plural of Targum) the Song of Song's Targum was likely used in situations in which audiences were unfamiliar with Hebrew, or at least unfamiliar enough with biblical Hebrew that it was necessary to translate to Aramaic. Because Aramaic is so closely related to Hebrew (the latter actually borrowed its alphabet from the former), the interpretation in the Targum engages in word play that is constantly in conversation with the Hebrew. This is significant because it serves to introduce perhaps the most important element of rabbinic interpretation: close reading with special attention to the verbal particularity and nuance of the text. Early rabbinic interpretation, in Hebrew and Aramaic, is remarkable for its attention to detail and its insight on the slightest nuance of language. Of course, as we shall see, this attentiveness leads to rather fanciful interpretations at times but, nonetheless, with proper filtering, the rabbis' insights are invaluable. More important, one can glean from their insights the conceptual frameworks that guide them. In many ways, this conceptual world is their inheritance from the texts they read. In other words, much of the way they understand the Song relates to their literary competence in picking up on the subtleties of the text. This emerges most clearly in the ways in which they read the Song as resonant not only with itself but also with other parts of the Hebrew Bible and, in particular, with the theology of love.

The Targum reads the Song as Solomon's account of Israel's history from the exodus to the future rebuilding of the third temple. The significance of these historical markers will emerge in our discussion below. For now, it is important to point out that for the Targumists, the exodus represents the origin of the relationship between Israel and God.[2] The rabbis inherit this understanding from several of the prophets who view the exodus and wilderness wanderings (Exod 1–Deut 34) as the honeymoon for Israel with its newly espoused God (recall Hos 2:16-25; Ezek 16; and so on). This prophetic vision informs the Targum to the Song at every turn. For the authors of the Targum, the remarkable language of love in the Song marks the deep affection that emerges between Israel and its God beginning with the exodus.

The Targum begins by explaining the repetition of the word *song* in the first verse (and title), "The Song of Songs which is Solomon's." Linguists have long recognized that the title "Song of Songs" is the means by which biblical Hebrew expresses the superlative "the best of songs." The rabbis, however, believed that Scripture never wasted words. In their opinion, the title suggested that this was the best song among a number of others— ten to be exact.[3] The Targum lists the ten songs, beginning with a quote from Ps 92:1, put in the mouth of Adam, and ending with a reference to a future tenth song that Israel will sing when it returns to Jerusalem and worships God at Zion. The intervening songs that the Targum cites are understood to come from various important points in the history of Israel. It is worth running through the list of the songs and highlighting the more significant ones. By doing so, it is possible to gain a sense of the interpretive strategy implied by the association of the Song of Songs with these other songs. Moreover, the subtlety of these associations reveals not only the ingenuity of the interpreters, but also the resonance within the texts with which they deal.

The first Song that the Targum cites is found in Ps 92. It reads: "A Psalm, a Song for the Sabbath." The rabbis take this Song to have been uttered by Adam when he received his pardon from God in the garden of Eden. While Christians viewed the events in the garden as the "fall" of Adam, many early Jewish interpreters viewed them quite differently. The latter recognized that while God threatened Adam with death for eating the forbidden fruit, when Adam and Eve actually did eat of it, they were merely chastised and exiled from the garden rather than killed. The early interpreters saw this as the first of numerous gracious acts of God. Moreover, they associated Ps 92 with the expression of Adam's relief at being pardoned from his rightful punishment. Why the rabbis believed that it was uttered about the Sabbath is complicated but relies on the association of Sabbath with rest and redemption generally and, perhaps, on some interpretations that viewed the events of the garden to have taken place on the sixth day of creation (*Pesiq. Rab Kah.* 23:1). This would mean that Adam recited Ps 92 the next day or on the Sabbath. Whatever the reason for the association of Adam and the Sabbath, the association of the psalm with Adam suggests that the rabbis understood the significance of the Song of Songs against the broad sweep of the history of all of mankind rather than in terms of Israelite history alone. Most significantly, they see in Ps 92 a reference to redemption that is in keeping with their reading of the Song of Songs. Moreover, by reading Ps 92 as a reference to the garden of Eden, they reveal that it, like the Song, reflects the ideal of divine intimacy.

The second song on the interpreters' list is that of Moses and Miriam found in Exod 15 where they and the rest of the Israelites celebrate their liberation and the destruction of the Egyptians. Significantly, the "Song of the Sea," as Exod 15:1-19 is called, ends with a reference to the culmination of God's great act:

> You will bring and plant your people on your mountain, the place you built to dwell in, O Lord. The sanctuary of my Lord, the work of your own hands. The Lord rules forever and ever. (Exod 15:17-18 AT)

By citing the Song of the Sea, and this verse in particular, the rabbis signal that the exodus event is merely prologue to the ultimate destiny of the Israelites; as in the Song of the Sea, the Jews will, in the end, celebrate when they return to the mountain of God and worship at his holy mountain where they will sing what the interpreters understand to be the tenth in their list of great biblical love songs. Of significance in verses 17-18 is that while the exodus culminated in the Israelites' arrival at Sinai, this passage suggests the association of that great mountain with Zion, the temple mount. We will see this association on a number of occasions in the Targum.

The six songs that the Targum identifies as three through eight in the series of the Bible's "top-ten" include the following: (three) Num 21:17-18; (four) Deut 32:1-43; (five) Josh 10:12-13; (six) Judg 5:1-31; (seven) 1 Sam 2:1-10; and (eight) 2 Sam 22:1-51. These songs all share the motif of Israel's (or a representative member's) celebration of deliverance in one form or another. The Numbers passage celebrates God's provision of a well in the wilderness. The Targum likely understands this event in light of the growing bond between Israel and God. In the text from Deuteronomy (song 4), Moses praises God's great might while recalling the events of the exodus (Deut 32:10-12). In Josh 10, Joshua himself utters the song that requests that the sun stand still so that Israel might defeat its enemy. For the Targumist, this prayer, no doubt, was one more bit of evidence that God was ever vigilant over Israel. The sixth song in the Targum's list is that sung by Deborah and Barak when Israel was delivered from General Sisera of Hazor. Song seven composes Hannah's prayer when she turns her son Samuel over to Eli the priest. Finally, song eight is David's praise of the Lord for deliverance from enemies. Of interest in this list is that their sequence follows that of the Hebrew Bible as we have it. By citing this sequence of songs, the Targum suggests that song represents the appropriate idiom for praising God's kindness to Israel. It is in this context that the Song of Songs is understood as the best among these songs that speak of the ongoing relationship between God, God's people, and his repeated deliverance of them. Significantly, like the other songs on the list, the Song of Songs represented to our interpreters a condensed version of their history with God.

The Song of Songs is actually listed as the ninth of the ten great songs sung "in this world." According to the Targum, the last of the songs will be sung by Israel when it is redeemed from exile (*be'idan deyifqun miggaluta'*). The Targum apparently paraphrases Isa 30:29 when it quotes the words of its tenth song:

> This will be your song of joy, like the night that is sanctified for the Passover Festival. And like the joy of the heart of the people who went to appear in front of the Lord three times per year with instruments of song and the sound of bells; in order to go to the mountain of the Lord to worship before the might of Israel.

Significantly, the Targum apparently takes this passage to refer to the future from the rabbis' perspective as well as Isaiah's. For them, the text in Isaiah alludes to the tenth and final song of Israel when it is reunited with its God in the final and lasting consummation of their relationship. There are several important points to make about the Targum's interpretation at this juncture. First, the paraphrase of the Isaiah passage is expansive beyond the Hebrew and is at variance with the Targum to Isaiah. Of most significance, the passage above gives a name to the otherwise unnamed festival in Isa 30:29. By identifying the festival as Passover (which marks the beginning of the exodus), the Targum takes advantage of the reference at the end of the passage to the "mountain of the Lord." The juxtaposition of the Passover and exodus motif with the reunion with God at his mountain makes this future event the fulfillment of the relationship between Israel and God, the culmination of which mirrors its origin in the distant past (Exod 15:17-18). Note that, again, Sinai and Zion are apparently viewed as one in this instance. Of most importance in this reading of the Targum is the realization that it understands the Song of Songs in this trajectory that everywhere presumes the exodus as the time in which Israel was first courted by God. In the midst of this tradition of song-making in the Bible, it is little wonder that the Targum takes the Song of Songs as the most supreme and indeed, most explicit song in the repertoire. As of the date of the composition of the Targum, the Song of Songs represents the greatest song of redemption in the Hebrew Bible.

Thus begins the Targum's treatment of the Song of Songs. By a clever reading of the significance of the term *Song of Songs*, the Targum signals that it views the Song in the context of this long history of song production, the goal of which had always been the praise of God and his wondrous acts of salvation. Significantly, this interpretive move also views the Song in the context of the rest of what the rabbis knew as Scripture. It is against the traditions known to them in the Bible that the Targum understands the Song's meaning. In their interpretation of Song 1:1, this understanding primarily revolves around the frequent occurrence of songs in the Hebrew Bible that are used to celebrate God's greatness. Some of the songs have closer thematic or even lexical associations with the Song as well. This multifarious interpretive perspective, one that recognizes associations among texts on several different counts, is characteristic of the rest of the Targum, rabbinic interpretation, and, indeed, much of premodern readings of the Bible. Guided by an ingenious associative logic, this type of reading recognizes the slightest similarity and seeks to expose its significance. While this method of interpretation can be far from any plain sense of a text, it often provides stunning insight into the literary and conceptual building blocks that form and inform the biblical text.

1:2

The Targum to verse 2 of the Song is a good example of how far from the plain sense its interpretation can be. It is an equally good example of the broader context in which early Jewish interpretation understood the Song. Recall verse 2 in the Bible: "Let him kiss me with the kisses of his mouth, for your love is better than wine." In the Aramaic of the Targum, this verse is understood to refer to the Lord who gave to Israel the Torah, Mishnah, and the Talmud. The Targum further understands the reference to kisses as the means by which God associated with Israel "face-to-face" ('*appin be'appin*), as one who kisses his beloved. This interpretation of the Song's second verse presupposes a common rabbinic understanding of the source of their sacred literature. According to *m. Abot* 1:1-18 the rabbis could trace the generations through which this literature passed from Moses down to their own time. Central to their understanding is that the written Torah, the Pentateuch as we know it, was only part of what God communicated to Moses at Sinai. In addition to this written Torah, there was an oral Torah that Moses did not have time to write down. This oral Torah eventually took written form and comprised the Mishnah and Talmud. The Targum, by associating the kisses with the face-to-face meeting of Moses with God, presumes that the Song of Songs celebrates that original meeting between Moses and God. Furthermore, it associates their sacred Scripture with the means by which Israel and rabbinic Judaism maintains this relationship, so intimate that it is understood to be like two people kissing.

Two things, in particular, are striking in the Targum's treatment of the Song of Songs thus far. First, we have noted most recently that the Targum links the kissing of 1:2 in the Song with the receiving of the Torah. This is especially interesting if we consider the verbal pun suggested by the wording of the original Hebrew text of 1:2. The verb for kissing (*n-sh-q*) is so similar to the verb for "to drink" (*sh-q-h*) that we are likely to recognize that the kissing is linked with the drinking of wine of the second half of the verse. That is to say, there is in the kissing an allusion to enjoying the love that is better than wine. One is to drink it all in, as it were. This wordplay in the Song may suggest that the Targum's interpretive stratagem is more sophisticated than one first suspects. Recall one of the two main trajectories of the theology of love in the Second Temple period, the Torah, came to be associated with the fertility and life-sustaining qualities of water. This association may find its (mostly inchoate) origins as early as the narratives of Exodus, but certainly can be seen in places like Sir 24 and many others. It seems quite plausible that this kind of assumption guides the Targum's interpretation of verse 2 of the Song. On this understanding, the Targum associates the kissing with the meeting of Moses with God. Moreover, the Torah itself is understood to be not only better than wine, but also as delightful to the palate. In this way, the double entendre of verse 2 of the Song is carried over into the Targum to become a doubled double entendre. Moses is understood to have received the Torah (living waters) through the kisses/drinking of the mouth. If this reading of the Targum is correct, it is truly a stunning interpretive move. It views the intimacy of that first encounter of God and Moses as perpetuated in the ongoing learning (read "kissing and drinking") of the Torah.

The second striking element in the Targum's treatment of the first two verses is in its presumption that the Song is making oblique reference to the temple (v. 1) and the Torah (v. 2). This likely reflects the trend in late Second Temple Judaism that associated Sinai, the mountain where Moses received the Torah, and Zion, the mountain where the temple resided. Indeed, as noted above, this trend can be traced in the biblical texts themselves.[4] These two mountains serve as the focal points of Israel's relations with God; it is both the temple and Torah that provide the two main thrusts of the theology of love that we are tracing herein. We point out the Targum's reading of verses 1 and 2 because it represents in very condensed form an example of the degree to which the association of the Torah and temple with the theology of love had gained ascendancy in the late antique world. The association is so much a part of their world that they understand the very introduction to the Song, in its first two verses, to be about the founding of the temple and the giving of the Torah. The Targum presupposes this association to the degree that they need not (perhaps even could not) articulate it.

1:3

While the first two verses of the Targum recognize and take advantage of some of the wordplay in the Song of Songs, their main interest lay in the elaboration of the mountain motifs outlined above. With the third verse of the Song, the Targum continues its association of the Song with the exodus but turns more of its attention to the aesthetic beauty of the language employed. In order to show the way in which the Targum reads verse 3, it is useful to cite the first three verses of the biblical book in their entirety:

The Song of Songs which is Solomon's.
Let him kiss me with the kisses of his mouth,
For your love is better than wine, the fragrance of your oils too.
Oil poured out is your name, therefore all the girls love you.

The Targum translates verse 3 as follows:

> At the sound of the your wonders and great works that you did for your
> people, the house of Israel, all the people shook; especially those who
> heard [*di shma'u*] the report [*shema'*] of your greatness and your good
> signs. Your holy name [*shmakh*] was heard ['*ishtema'*] in all the world as
> more choice than the abundant anointing [*mimeshakh*] that was placed
> upon the heads of kings and priests. As a result, the righteous desired to
> follow after your good ways in order to gain this world ['*alma' haden*]
> and the world to come ['*alma' de' ate*].

The Targum's rendering of the third verse continues to reveal the
translators' keen literary sensitivity and the imagination with which they
interpret the Song. The exquisitely crafted Hebrew of verse 3 is worth
reproducing.

> *lereakh shemanekha tovim*
> *shemen turaq shemekha*
> *'al-ken 'alamot 'ahevukha*

> The fragrance of your oils (is better than wine) too,
> Oil poured out is your name,
> Therefore all the girls love you.

The Hebrew itself puns on the similar sounds in the words
shemanekha (your oil), *shemen* (oil), and *shemekha* (your name). This
assonance serves to reinforce the sensuous nature of the subject at hand
as well as to suggest the multiple senses that are involved, including sight,
smell, taste, and even hearing. The Targum is alert to the same quality of
the language in its interpretation of this verse. For the Targumists, the
Hebrew nouns *shemanekha*, *shemen*, and *shemekha* suggest the Aramaic
version's hearing (*shema'u*) of the report (*shema'*) about God. Moreover,
the Targum insists that the hearing ('*ishtema'*) of the divine name
(*shmakh*) is better than anointing oil (*mimeshakh*).[5] The Targum, again,
picks up on and extends the wordplay suggested by the Hebrew. Whereas
the Hebrew Song merely alludes to the sense of hearing in its version (the

sound of the oil poured out), the Targum makes the hearing explicit; but this hearing is understood to take place in the context of language that is thoroughly reminiscent of the exodus and conquest narratives in Exodus and Joshua. Once again, the motif of the exodus and its attendant themes emerges in the Targum's translation.

The Targum attempts to improve and, perhaps elaborate, on the Hebrew by mimicking its style, when it shifts to the word *meshakh* (anointing oil) to translate the Hebrew *shemen* (oil). This subtle shift is nice because the first two consonants of the Aramaic word are the same (albeit reversed) as those of the Hebrew. Moreover, *mutatis mutandis*, it sounds much like the Hebrew term *shemekha* (your name). The interpreters, thus, hear in the "oil (*meshakh*) poured out" the name (*shmakh*) of God. Further, the notion of "oil poured out" is suggestive of the sound and smell of anointing. But the cleverness of this shift only becomes clear when we see that it also serves to tie the last third of verse 3 to the first two thirds. To understand how it does this, we need to consider the pun the Targum makes on the Hebrew word for *girls* (*ʿalamot*) in the last third of verse 3. Whereas the Hebrew says, "Therefore all the girls love you," the Targum reads: "As a result, the righteous desired to follow after your good ways in order to gain this world and the world to come." The Targum, using the same root (*ʿ-l-m*) as that for girls (*ʿalamot*) in the Hebrew, changes to the word for world (*ʿalmaʾ*). By so doing, the Targum apparently reads the last part of verse 3 to mean, "Those who love you do so on account of the world to come." That is, they who love you do so in order to have a share in the world to come; but their share in the world to come is also a result of their love for God. What makes this reading so fascinating is the Hebrew Bible's designation of kings as messiah, *mashiakh* in Hebrew. Moreover, by the late Second Temple period the *mashiakh* came to be associated with the future redemption of Israel (cf. Jer 23:1-4; Ezek 17:22-24; and so on). It appears that the Targum uses the Aramaic *meshakh* to translate *shemen* because it sees in the hearing (*ʾishtemaʿ*) of God's name (*shmakh*), even in the exodus, a foreshadowing of his future redemption in the world to come. By employing the word *meshakh* the Targum ties all of verse 3 together (by its "future" association with the root *ʿ-l-m*) while tying it to the larger exodus/redemption theme that drives their understanding of the Song. Finally it is important to point out that the use of *meshakh* also suggests that the Targum wanted to establish a stronger link between Song 1:3 and 1:4. In order to explain this last claim, we need to turn to the latter.

1:4

Verse 4 of the Song reads:

> Draw me after you, let us run!
> The king has brought me to his chambers.
> Let us delight and rejoice in your love,
> Savoring it more than wine-
> Like new wine they love you.

The Targum takes this verse to refer directly to the events of the exodus. According to their translation, the Israelites are quoted on their departure from Egypt (led by the divine presence) as follows:

> Master of the world (*'alma'*), let us be drawn after you, and follow your good way. Bring us near to the base of Mount Sinai and give us the Torah from your storehouse which is in heaven. We shall celebrate and be glad in the twenty-two letters with which they are written. We shall remember them and desire your divinity; separating ourselves from the presence of the idols of other people. All the righteous who serve firmly before you will fear you and desire your commandments.

Clearly, the Targum has treated the Hebrew rather loosely and represents a considerably expanded account. Of particular interest are the ways that the Targum continues to pick up and expand on the wordplay of the original as well as the ways in which it continues to view the Song in light of the exodus.

The wordplay here continues with the invocation of God as "master of the world." Of course, the word for world is the by now familiar *'alma'* By repeating the term, the Targum recalls its use in verse 3 (in the Targum) and again suggests the connection between the redemption in the world to come with the one that took place at the exodus. But the Targum does not stop there. It seems that the Targumists recognize that the Hebrew imperative verb *moshkheni* ("draw me") that is found in first position of verse 4 provides a transition from the main sonal element of the first three verses to what follows. The first two consonants of this imperative compose the (reversed) sonal elements that dominated the first three verses of the book in Hebrew (*sh, m, q, k*). Moreover, it seems quite possible that they further tie verses 3 and 4 together proleptically in verse 3 when they used the term *meshakh*; note how much it sounds like *moshkheni.* By employing *meshakh* in verse 3 the Targum puns on the Hebrew imperative of verse 4 and suggests the association between the anointed of verse 3 and the king of verse 4.

As for the exodus theme, the text could hardly be more explicit in fixing this association. The "drawing after" of the Hebrew now comes out of the mouth of Israel who seeks to be in God's presence. Moreover, the image of the king bringing his lover to his room is understood by the Targum to refer to Israel's intimate contact with God at Sinai where the Torah was provided from the divine "treasury." As a result of God's granting this request, Israel will serve God and follow his commandments.

Summary of the Targum to Song of Songs 1:1-4

Even from this very brief investigation of the Targum's treatment of the Song, the modus operandi emerges quite clearly. First, the Targumists are acutely aware of the literary beauty and subtlety of the Song. Their translation consistently presumes and often expands on this quality of the text. Their literary competence lies at a number of levels, however. For instance, they are very attuned to the verbal gamesmanship of the Song. They signal their awareness in their recognition and expansion of the puns on words containing the consonants *sh, m, q,* and *k* that dominate the first four verses of the original, Hebrew Song. In their expansions on the wordplay, they manage to suggest connections between the verses that are absent in the Hebrew original. Furthermore, they also suggest, or perhaps presume, allusions to other texts that the original does not. In particular, they persistently interpret the Song as a subtle allusion to the exodus and Israel's earliest redemption. It is through this association that the Targum sees in the Song the celebration of Israel's relationship with God.

Most interesting in the Targum's presumption of the sacrality of the Song and its subject is the way they assume the unity of its aesthetic and divine nature. The wonderful sound of the Song is understood as an integral part of its meaning. The puns themselves are recognized to convey as much as the content of their verbal references. While the Hebrew celebrates the delightful assonance of its vocabulary and implies a world of sensual pleasure, the Targum expands on this aesthetic by echoing the redemptive tones of the Hebrew original. The profound and overwhelming realm of the senses suggests to the Targumists the climax of their corporate religious lives, God's former and future redemption. Significantly, it is not only the sonal quality of the Hebrew that the Targum picks up on but also its metaphoric repertoire.

While the Targum seems to ignore, or perhaps to presume, the human poignancy of the sexual metaphors of the Song, it clearly sees in them a divine reflection. The kisses are none other than God's communication to Moses. The oil poured out is understood to have two distinct but related aspects. It suggests God's name is more delightful than both the sound and fragrance of fine oil. Especially remarkable is the chamber of love of the Song that, in the Targum, is the treasure house of the Torah in heaven.

At every turn, the Targum sees in the Song's rich and sensual language the divine. For the Targumists, the sacrality of the Song is embedded in its sounds, metaphors, and erotic aesthetic. From their perspective, there was no other way for the Song to tell of Israel's great love affair with God. Text, words, sounds, syllables, even the fragrance of love are all part of the profound sacrality of the Song for the Targum. There is no separation between these bodily and divine pleasures that they connote. God's love for his people is built into the very aesthetic of the text itself. For the Targumists, the sounds of the Song merely echo the other sensual pleasures embodied in the text.

This necessarily brief discussion of the Targum's treatment of the Song serves well to introduce the history of the interpretation of the Song. In the first place, the history of the early interpretation that we are tracing in this, part 2, of our study consistently responds to the stunning beauty of the poetic language and imagery of the Song. It does this by paying very close attention to the verbal particularity of the text. Each sound, syllable, word, or even phrase or clause is heard against a tradition within which it resonates. Much like the Song itself must be understood by means of its resonance within its various parts, the history of interpretation understands it in relation to Scripture writ large. As we have seen above, the Targum often takes its lead from the Song itself when it extends its wordplay and interprets the Song in a larger literary context. This is characteristic of the other two examples of early interpretation that we shall consider below.

Of note, the Targum to the first four verses is representative of the way it treats the rest of the Song. Here too, for the Targum, the Song is a poetic rendition of the exodus and wilderness wandering that compose the honeymoon of Israel and God. It is likely not an accident that this mimics the fact that Exod 15 represents a poetic version of the events depicted in Exod 14.[6] In other words, the interpreters understand the Song to mimic the function of Exod 15, only in this case, the Song is the ultimate example of a poetic rendition of God's redemption. The interpreters understand the exodus as precursor to the final future redemption alluded to in the Song.

In addition to understanding the Song as a poetic and condensed version of God's history of redemption, early Jewish interpretation seems also to read the Song in the genre of historical recitation as a reminder of covenant obligations. All such passages are too numerous to list fully, but examples come from places like Deut 26:5-10a; Josh 24; Ps 78; and so on. This last passage is especially revealing for how early Jewish interpretation understood the Song. While Ps 78 recites God's remarkable history with his people, in verses 56-64 we hear of the devastating consequences of the failure of Israel to observe their covenantal obligations. In the conclusion to the Psalm in verses 65-72, however, we read of an awakened God who comes to the aid of his people and, once again, tends them as a good shepherd. To the degree that early Jewish interpretation reads the Song as part of this kind of historical recitation, it deals directly with a tragic history by suggesting that the Song, like the conclusion to Ps 78, envisages redemption; but for readers of the Song, it is the final and lasting redemption.

Read as part of the genre of historical recitation, early interpreters likely also heard in the Song resonance with several instances in the Bible where God needs to be reminded of his own covenantal obligations. Psalm 78 is one example, but we could add, among others, Pss 74 and 79. It seems likely that these Jewish readers viewed the Song in the context of this type of psalm as well, which is, after all, merely a historical recitation of God's need, on occasion, to be reminded to act on behalf of his people. That this understanding of the Song resonates with depictions of Moses in Exod 32, where he defends the Israelites after the episode of the golden calf, reinforces all the more how much the Song is deeply in conversation with the rest of their Scripture. For these early interpreters, no matter the doubt instilled by a painful present, the Song of Songs represents a love song in which both lovers are reminded of a past that serves as a promise for a bright future.

This reading of the Song in such profoundly moving theological terms in the Targum is representative of Jewish interpretation of the Song in general, as our discussion of the midrashim on the first four verses of the Song will reveal. We next turn to the collection known as *Midrash Rabbah* on the Song of Songs to gain a sense of the variety of early Jewish interpretation. After considering *Midrash Rabbah* to the Song, we shall turn to Origen as an example of early Christian interpretation of the Song's significance. All of this will serve to reveal the profound sacral significance the Song had for its early interpreters. For all concerned, the Song is nothing if not the greatest of the songs that celebrate God's eternal vigilance and devotion.

CHAPTER FIVE

MIDRASH RABBAH TO SONG OF SONGS 1:1-4

As noted above, the dating of much of rabbinic literature is complicated by the nature of its production and preservation. This is as true of the midrash to Song of Songs as it is of the Targum. Again, because midrash represents a compilation of comments from a rather extended period of time, discussion of its date has to be carefully nuanced. Most would accept that most of the material in our midrash came together by the eighth century C.E. As with the Targum to the Song, however, it must be conceded that there is much in the midrash that comes from very early in the history of its interpretation. Our goal, as in the preceding chapter, is merely to use the midrash as an example of the ways in which the Song was received in rabbinic Judaism. The dating of the interpretations is less significant than gaining an understanding of the interpretive assumptions brought to the Song. We shall see that they are much like those of the Targum.

Before starting our investigation of the midrash, it is important to note how selective we must be. The commentary on just the first four verses of the Song takes up roughly twenty-eight pages in a Hebrew edition and around fifty-five pages in a popular English translation.[1] Clearly, we could not reproduce all of *Song of Songs Rabbah*, let alone provide any extended discussion of it. A further note is in order for those unfamiliar with the rabbinic exegesis known as midrash. In the first place, it is highly dependent, like the Targum we have just considered, on the verbal particularity of the biblical text. It often is interested in a specific word, image, metaphor, or motif, and the ways that any one of these elements resonates with the rest of Jewish Scripture. As a result of this characteristic, midrashic interpretation often seems so particularistic that one can hardly draw any generalization from its observations. Moreover, midrash is given to investigating recurrences of the specific literary elements listed above wherever they occur. This leads to what often seem to be considerable digressions. In the following we shall select examples of the midrash and seek to represent the general tone of the work rather than to be exhaustive in our coverage. Furthermore, we will not pursue every digression or avenue taken by the midrash even though this would give a better sense of the discursive nature of its commentary.

1:1

The very first midrash in *Song Rab.* 1 is instructive of the way early interpreters came to understand the Song and its significance. In explaining the initial superlative construction "The Song of Songs," the rabbis say, "This is what scripture says through Solomon: 'Watch the man busy at his work, he stands before Kings, not before brooding men' " (quoting Prov 22:29). The reasons the rabbis cite this verse are, as one might expect, multiple and complex. First, they go to another text ascribed to Solomon and, in the process, address the unspoken question, "What are the other songs suggested by the title 'Song of Songs'?" Furthermore, characteristic of so much midrash, this one cites only one verse, Prov 22:29, but has in mind a larger literary context. Notably, Prov 22:20, just nine verses before the one they cite, says: "Have I not written for you 'three times' (*shalishiwm*) in wise counsel?"[2] Here, the rabbis understand the reference to "three times" to be the three books traditionally ascribed to Solomon; Proverbs, Qohelet (Ecclesiastes), and Song of Songs. Moreover, they see embedded in the book of Proverbs a reference from Solomon to these three books with which he busied himself.

While the Proverbs passage is initially cited to illumine the first verse of the Song, the rabbis next turn to a discussion of the Proverbs verse itself. In so doing, they appear to resolve the obscure reference in the verse but, at a much more subtle level, continue their commentary on the Song as well. We need to consider carefully the ways in which they do this. The first obscurity that they attempt to resolve is best formulated in a question: *Who is the one who is "busy at his work" (bimla'khto) in Prov*

22:29? Like nearly all midrash, ours presumes its question without explicitly articulating it. In order to answer this question, the rabbis turn to a passage in which the word for "his work" also appears, Gen 39:11, which reads, "He came into the house in order to do his work" (*mela'khto*). These represent two of the fourteen occurrences of this word in the Hebrew Bible.[3] The rabbis imply that the reference in Prov 22:29 must be to Joseph, the subject of Gen 39, who was "busy at his work." They go on to claim that Gen 39:11 makes reference to a festival day on which no one but Joseph and Potiphar's wife was present in the house. This explains why Joseph and his boss's wife were alone in the house together. But what is the significance of the reference to Joseph being "busy at his work"? In answer to this (unspoken) question, the rabbis imply that because of his unyielding devotion to his master and his work, Joseph was able to go free. The rabbis likely have in mind that although Joseph was jailed on Mrs. Potiphar's accusations, he did eventually go free (Gen 40–41). For the rabbis, the significance of Joseph's dedication to his work is that it kept him chaste in relation to Potiphar's wife.[4] This chastity, in turn, is viewed as a sign of Joseph's righteousness and dedication to God. As a result of this loyalty and righteousness, Joseph is finally set free.

Apparently, the midrash understands the events of Joseph's life to adumbrate the exodus itself where Israel's loyalty is understood constantly to be tested and made the condition of the continued presence of God (cf. Exod 32 and 33). On the rabbis' reading, the Joseph account is merely a condensed variation on the exodus theme. In this, one must admire their literary competence. Moreover, they likely understand all too well the recurring nature of the theme embedded in this scenario. Theirs was a long history of oppression accompanied by the hope that righteousness might influence their fate. While their commentary on Prov 22 takes them to Gen 39 ostensibly to solve the puzzle of who is "busy at his work," in Gen 39 they pick a passage that, on their reading, resonates with the theme of the Song of Songs and the theology of love in general: chastity or sexual loyalty to God is the prerequisite for freedom. Just as the rabbis view the Song as referring to the events of the exodus from Egypt, they pick a passage in Genesis that is about the prototypical ancestor whose willingness to resist temptation leads to freedom. One must note the degree to which the rabbis presume the prophetic idiom in which apostasy and adultery were one and the same thing. Joseph's ability to resist adultery (read "apostasy") proved that he merited freedom. For the midrash, the celebration of the relationship between Israel and God in sexual metaphor is the marker of the proper relations between these two old lovers. It, like Joseph's early example, is marked by the resistance to temptation and dedication to one's duty.

However tentative it must remain, it seems that something like this reading informs our midrash on the first verse of the Song. By citing Prov 22:29, the rabbis, as usual, make an amazing set of associations that are at once verbal, motivic, visual, and theological. They see in the story of Joseph a foreshadowing of the theme of the Song of Songs. More impressive, they see in Prov 22:29 Solomon's allusion to this common theme. As we proceed, we shall see over and again this fundamental and constitutive characteristic of midrashim—the citing of a text that, on first glance, seems so remote as to be of little value. On further consideration, however, we discover the subtlety and sophistication of the associations that underlie most of the rabbis' textual citations.

After supplying the previous solution to the problem of "the one busy at his work," another Darshan (the rabbinic teacher who creates midrashim) provides another interpretation (*davar 'akher*) in *Song Rab.* 2. "The one busy at his work" is none other than Moses himself. This identification, again, is based on the rabbis' reading of Prov 22:29, but this time they see an important verbal association with the middle third of the verse, which reads: "he stands before kings" (*lifne melakhim yityatsav*). To make the connection to Moses the rabbis cite Exod 8:16, which reads (in part): "The Lord said to Moses, 'Get up early in the morning and stand before Pharaoh [*hityatsev lifne parʿoh*].'" So for the rabbis, the one who is busy at his work and stands before the king is Moses, just as the text of Exod 8:16 attests. The rabbis, once again, depend on the verbal similarity between the Proverbs text and the proof-text in Exodus. Note the similarity in phrasing between the two passages they cite. At a deeper level, this midrash likely also has in mind the association between Moses as leader of the exodus and the fact that the Song is understood to celebrate the love of God for Israel that began with the exodus. Moreover, they likely associate the notion of one going free, which was stated explicitly in the first midrash, with Moses. In other words, Moses was busy at his work, stood before a king, and, in the end, went free. In fact, it was because of his showdown with Pharaoh that Moses and Israel did originally go free. Again, the rabbis see in Prov 22:29 Solomon's allusion to the connection between the exodus and the Song.

Song of Songs Rabbah 3 suggests that "he who is busy at his work" (Prov 22:29 AT) refers to the righteous "who are busy with the work of the Holy one, Blessed be he." That work is defined by explaining the second third of Prov 22:29, "he stands before kings" (*lifne melakhim yityatsav*), by reference to another passage in Proverbs, 8:15, where we read, "Through me kings rule, Rulers make righteous statutes." The midrash explains that to stand before the king is to "stand firmly in the Torah" (*mityatsevim battorah*). The linkage in this interpretation is subtle. They begin by presuming, with Sirach, that the speaker in Prov 8:15, Wisdom, is none other than Torah. In so doing, they assert that Prov 8:15 fills in the obscure reference in Prov 22:29 to "standing before a king" by explaining that it is through the Torah that kings rule. Therefore, standing before a king is the same as standing firm in the Torah. Recall that early Jewish interpretation, including those interpreters of our midrash, followed Sirach's lead in viewing Prov 8 as an extended treatment of the Torah and its role at the beginning of creation. By citing chapter 8, the midrash suggests that Solomon's literary production in Proverbs can be read in concert with the Song. In this way, the rabbis apparently understand Solomon to be making a link between the Torah and what they view as the main theme of the Song, the exodus. Of course, as noted above, the rabbis may merely see this linkage as part of the divine literary plan rather than the intention of Solomon, but that they associate the Proverbs passages and the Torah with the Song and its supposed exodus theme is clear. Of course, it is after the exodus that Israel receives the Torah. Moreover, note that we have seen already in the Targum the association of the Song with the giving of the Torah (see commentary on *Tg. Song* 1:2 above).

Recall that in our discussion of the Targum to the first four verses we pointed out that the interpreters see in the Song a reference to both the Torah and the temple. It is, therefore, not surprising that the next two chapters of the midrash, *Song Rab.* 4–5, view Song 1:1 in light of the temple. Once again, the interpreters explain the first clause of Prov 22:29 in relation to the Song. In chapter 4 they claim that "he who is busy at his work" is Rabbi Hanina. They tell the story of the rabbi who, on seeing his fellow citizens taking whole-burnt ('*olot*) and peace (*shelamim*) offerings to Jerusalem (read "the temple"), realized he had not the means to do the same. We are told the remarkable story of how he went out into the countryside and found a rock that he polished, painted, and then brought, with the help of fifty angels, to Jerusalem. This is a typical rabbinic tale (Aggadah) about one of their cohorts. While the story is fascinating in its own right, of most interest is the association of the "one busy at his work" with one who makes a vow to make an (albeit unusual) offering to the Lord. The midrash here is especially discursive in its insistence on telling the story of Rabbi Hanina, but its association of the Song with the temple, while oblique, is nonetheless important. In chapter 5 this same association is made with a much more familiar, indeed a biblical, character.

Song of Songs Rabbah 5 explains that the "one busy at his work" in Prov 22:29 is Solomon himself. More specifically, it addresses what the rabbis view as a rather scandalous detail in the account of Solomon's building of the temple and his own palace. The midrash cites 1 Kgs 6:38 where it says that Solomon spent seven years building the temple. In the very next verse, 1 Kgs 7:1, the text records that Solomon spent thirteen years building his palace. Naturally, the interpreters are anxious about this information; they presume the question, "Should not Solomon have spent much more time on the temple than on his own residence?" For the darshanim, the answer to this conundrum comes from Solomon's own mouth, or hand, when he hints in Prov 22:29 that he is the "one busy at his work." In other words, the interpreters understand the reference in Proverbs to be Solomon's defense against the charge that he spent nearly twice as much time on his palace as on the temple; he was simply much more diligent in his efforts on the temple.

There is one final interesting aside in all of this. In the discussions of the details of building the temple, the interpreters suggest that the temple built itself. They make this claim based on subtle distinctions in the language used in the accounts of building the temple found in 1 Kgs 6–8. They spend a considerable amount of time discussing the ways in which the stones of the temple were set, and in one case Rabbi Berekiah claims that the "stones lifted themselves up and placed themselves on the wall" (*hayetah ha'eben nose't 'et 'atsmah wenittenah 'al gabbe haddimos*). Two things, in particular, are of interest in this interpretation. First, recall that in *Song Rab.* 4 we saw the story of the attempts by Rabbi Hanina to attain and embellish a stone as an offering for the Lord. Now in chapter 5 we see another midrash, this time about the building of the temple, that fixes on the image of stones that lift themselves into place. This tangential and oblique reference to stones in the two contiguous midrashim is characteristic of midrash. While the two accounts are hardly on the same interpretive trajectory, they somehow resonate and come to be placed next to one another in our collection. This brings us to the second point to be made about the juxtaposition of these two midrashim. Both associate the first verse of the Song with Prov 22:29 and both concentrate on the explicit and detailed imagery of stones that serve in the cultic sphere. More to the point, in *Song Rab.* 5 they associate the account of Solomon's building the temple in 1 Kings with Prov 22:29 and the Song. Again, the rabbis reveal the great importance of the temple in their theology of love. Almost by nature, and without explaining the path they take, the rabbis presume the centrality of the building of the temple in the maintenance of Israel's relations with God. Of course, this is especially poignant in the wake of its destruction in ca. 70 C.E. Furthermore, the midrash engages three texts, all of which they view as intimately associated with Solomon, and each of which they presume illumines the other. For them, Solomon hints at his crowning achievement of building the temple in Prov 22:29. Finally, the interpreters recall at the end of *Song Rab.* 5 that Solomon wrote three books, Proverbs, the Song of Songs, and Qohelet; all because the holy spirit rested (*sharetah*, a pun on *shir hashirim* or the Song of Songs) on Solomon.

In the first five chapters of *Song of Songs Rabbah*, we have encountered some familiar interpretive tacks. Much like the Targum to the Song of Songs, the midrash views the initial parts of the Song in light of the motifs of the exodus, Torah, and temple. In the instance of our midrash, the interpreters consistently turn to the same Proverbs passage to illumine these motifs. Of note, like all midrash, ours is able to see multiple meanings in a single verse of the Song. Moreover, it views these multiple meanings through the lens of the same Proverbs passage. This multivocal quality of our midrash is characteristic of nearly all early Jewish interpretation, which is able to hear multiple voices in the verbal and metaphorical subtleties of the Song. Of particular interest is the fact that the interpreters hear in these multiple voices not a cacophony of confusion and obscurity but, rather, the symphony of the complex interrelations between parts of Scripture. Once again, the early interpreters are alert to the rich interplay of the literary elements of the Song with the rest of Scripture. This attentiveness is evident in the rest of their interpretation of the Song as well.

We next turn to *Song Rab.* 7 where we are offered yet another interpretation of the phrase "The Song of Songs." Again, likely because of its supposed link to Solomon, the interpreters turn to Proverbs in order to illumine the opening phrase. This time, however, the midrash cites Prov 16:23 where we read: "The heart of the wise one teaches his mouth [*pihu*], he adds learning to his lips" (AT). The midrash next says that the heart of a wise man is full of wisdom but asks, "Who is it that teaches him and makes him wise?" The answer is, "His mouth (*pihu*) makes him wise and teaches him." There are two salient points in this interpretation. First, the interpreters essentially reverse the syntax of Prov 16:23 when they answer their own question; now it is the mouth that teaches the heart, rather than the opposite implied by Proverbs. Second, as one might expect, the choice of the particular verse in Proverbs is no accident. While they cite it to solve the initial phrase, it also has important resonance with Song 1:2, the very next verse of the Song, where we read: "Let him kiss me with the kisses of his mouth [*pihu*]!" The significance of this verbal connection is made clearer in the subsequent lines of the midrash where the interpreters address the second half of Prov 16:23.

It is the last half of Prov 16:23 that provides the interpreters with the key that unlocks the significance of the whole verse and, in particular, how it sheds light on the opening verse of the Song. The rabbis claim the true meaning of Prov 16:23 is "by the very act of bringing forth the words of Torah from his heart, he adds to the learning of the Torah." The midrash goes on to assert that it is Solomon who "brings forth the words of Torah from his heart" and "adds to the learning of the Torah." Several elements of this interpretation are fascinating. First, once again, we see the association of the Song with the Torah; in this instance the Song (as well as Proverbs and Qohelet) is understood as Solomon's "addition" to the Torah. Significantly, the verbal connection suggested by the occurrence of "his mouth" in Song 1:2 and Prov 16:23 also reveals a connection between the Song and the Torah. Of note, for the interpreters, "his mouth" in Song 1:2 refers to God's, while in Prov 16:23 it refers to Solomon's. The interpreters apparently hear in his plea to God for the "kisses of his mouth" Solomon's request for the wisdom to add to God's Torah through his (Solomon's) mouth. This detail of the interpretation relies on the story in 1 Kgs 3:4-15 where Solomon prays to God for wisdom. That prayer seems to be answered, at least in part, in 1 Kgs 5:9-12 where we are told that God granted Solomon wisdom and understanding to such a great extent that he wrote three thousand proverbs and one thousand and five songs. The interpreters take the Song of Songs to be one of those songs and, clearly, Proverbs to be filled with many of those proverbs. Beyond making the literary association between 1 Kings and their midrash, the interpreters also reveal what is a standard rabbinic understanding of Torah. While the Torah, that is the five Books of Moses, came directly from the kisses of God's mouth, Solomon's additions come from his (own) mouth. This is a shorthand version of the rabbinic doctrine of two Torah's: one that was given to and written by Moses and a secondary one that was given to Moses, passed on by word of mouth, and part of which they understand to have been recorded by Solomon in his three books. Significantly, this secondary Torah is known to the rabbis as the *torah she be ʿal peh*, the "oral Torah" or the "Torah which is by mouth." The interpreters hear in the reference to "his mouth" in both Proverbs and the Song a reference to what they know as the oral Torah.

Beyond displaying an interest in the two modes of Torah with which the rabbis were familiar, the midrash actively engages the language of the Song in much the same way that the Targum does. The interpreters of the midrash also recognize the rich and complex aesthetic of the Song and, in their interpretations, expand on it. In the process, they respond to and elaborate on the beautiful aural quality of the Song while associating it with another text understood to come from Solomon's mouth. The interpreters seem to hear in the splendid alliteration of the first two lines of the Song the sweet voice of God who, after all, gave the Torah to Israel in the first place. In this way, the rabbis reveal that the sacrality of the Song is embedded in its divine aesthetic as much as in its divine source, which are likely inseparable in their minds. This chapter of *Song of Songs Rabbah* does much to bolster our contention that the interpreters view the aesthetic quality of the Song to be of divine origin—indeed, it is from the mouth of God. Moreover, this appreciation for the sensuousness of the sounds of the Song is the first step in understanding the rest of the Song's sensuality as essentially divine as well. For the rabbis, the desire stirred in the audience of the Song would merely be the replication of desire described therein.

Song of Songs Rabbah 8 turns to yet another book ascribed to Solomon in order to explain the opening of Song of Songs. The rabbis cite Qoh 12:9, which reads: "Furthermore, because Qohelet was wise, he also taught the people knowledge and tested [*'izzen*], sought out, and arranged many proverbs" (AT). Of course, the rabbis understood that Qohelet was none other than Solomon, based on the first verse of the book, which claims that it comprises "the words of Qohelet, son of David, King of Jerusalem" (Qoh 1:1 AT). The interpreters see in Qoh 12:9 a hint of the role Solomon, and the Song of Songs in particular, play in interpreting the Torah. They do this, as one might expect, by means of close reading and imaginative interpretation. Specifically, they see in the verb *tested* an allusion to the early part of the Song. This is possible because the root for the verb, '-z-n, is also used in Hebrew for the noun ear ('ozen) and verbs that refer to hearing (he'ezin). The rabbis claim that the use of the root in Prov 12:9 suggests the audience is obliged to listen to Solomon's words. Given the aural beauty of the early part of the Song, it is clear why the rabbis would call for attentive listening to Solomon's words. The rabbis elaborate on the value of listening to Solomon on two fronts. First they say that it was he who "made handles" ('oznayim) for the Torah. Here the rabbis engage in a double pun, first in using a word that is very similar to the noun for ear and second by suggesting the notion of grasping the Torah. Both puns suggest the sensual quality of their appreciation of the Torah.

The second important reason for listening to Solomon, according to the midrash, is related to those already enumerated. The rabbis claim that "until Solomon came along, no one was able to understand the words of the Torah" ('ad shello' 'amad shelomoh lo' hayah 'adam yakhol lehaskil divre torah). They explain that Solomon provided the means by which one can plumb the depths of Scripture: these are the proverbs and other metaphoric tropes Solomon devised to reveal the "secret of the Torah" (sodah shel torah). Rabbi Hanina explains that this can be com-pared to a case in which there was a deep well full of water (liv'er 'amuqqah mele'ah mayim) that was cold, fresh, and tasty, but no one was able to drink from it. Then a fellow came along and provided rope tied to rope (khevel bekhevel) and string tied to string until it was long enough to draw water from the well and let people drink from it. Thus, Hanina says, "From one word to another, from one proverb to another, Solomon revealed the secrets of the Torah."

Several things are of interest in Hanina's little parable of the well. First, note that in his reference to the ropes that the man (understood as Solomon) joined, there is a pun on the opening of the book of Qohelet where we traditionally read "vanities of vanities" (hevel havalim, AT). Hanina apparently implies that the book of Qohelet itself is part of the means by which one is able to reach the "depths of the well" that is the Torah. More important than Hanina's pun is the realization that he asso-ciates the Torah, once again, with water imagery. Indeed, as we have seen, the association of the Torah with water is constitutive of the theology of love in the Second Temple period. Note the sensuous pleasures suggested by Hanina's interpretation. Not only does it make a subtle reference to the book of Qohelet, but it also does so with the imagery of drinking, which ties in so closely with all the liquid imagery that fills the first four verses of the Song. In fact, it seems to play off of not only the imagery in those verses, but even the fluid sounds that predominate.

Song of Songs Rabbah 8 has proved a rich source for illumining the rabbinic approach to the Song. Once again, we have seen in the interpretations the active response to the beauty of the original text. In response to its beautiful alliteration, the midrash elaborates on the notion of listening to the Torah. In response to the imagery and sensual pleasures of drinking in Song 1:2, the rabbis emphasize the notion of a well and its refreshment. Of course, there are other associations that come with invoking the parable of the well, including fertility and its further association with the Torah (recall Sir 24). Moreover, the aural and oral pleasures they respond to and elaborate are all related to the kisses of the mouth of Song 1:2. Most important is to recognize the degree to which the rabbis continue to articulate their understanding of the sanctity of the Song and its place in Scripture. For them, the intimacy and aesthetic of love in the Song are inseparable and equally divine. They hear in Solomon's words, both in the Song and in Qohelet, Solomon's call to listen carefully and appreciate their literary treasures. Moreover, in these two books, Solomon has provided the means to plumb the depths of the living waters that is Torah.

Song of Songs Rabbah 11 concludes the interpretation of the first verse of the Song. Of particular interest in this chapter is a discussion taken from *m. Yad.* 3:5 where several rabbis debate the sacrality of various books we now know as Scripture. Among the books they discuss is the Song of Songs. Rabbi Aqiba (mid-second century C.E.) supplies the comment that sums up his evaluation of the Song and, simultaneously, partakes in a consistent theme in the early interpretation of the Song. In reference to the Song, Aqiba is quoted as saying: "All the writings [the third division of the Hebrew Bible] are holy but this one is the holy of holies [*qodesh qodashim*]." In this final phrase Aqiba provides an insight that is as subtle as it is revealing about his cultural competence. First, he uses a term that is the syntactic equivalent of the name "Song of Songs." In doing so, he suggests that the title makes reference not just to its greatness among all songs but to its ultimate sanctity as well. Furthermore, Aqiba associates the Song with the most sacred and restricted area of the temple, the holy of holies. Aqiba seems to suggest that the Song is the equivalent of the holy of holies, understood by extension as the temple. This is significant on several levels. Recall that the temple was the traditional locus of God's presence in Israel. This is especially true of the holy of holies, which only the high priest was allowed to enter once a year. This restricted access reveals another subtlety suggested by Aqiba's comment. Access to the Song, as the marker of the union of God with his people, may be as limited as was access to the holy of holies. Indeed, he suggests its title alludes to just this quality of the Song. The difference between the holy of holies and the Song of Songs, Aqiba seems to imply, is that it is the interpreter who must now enter that sacred domain rather than the priest. Aqiba's remarks on the Song suggest the reality that Scripture, and especially the Song of Songs, could replicate the role of the temple as the locus of God's presence. In particular, it shows the centrality of the Song in Aqiba's understanding of how to maintain intimacy with God. In addition, Aqiba's comment may suggest that in his mind and in his world, the role of the interpreter was understood to replicate the former role of the priest in the sacred domain.

In our discussion of *Song Rab.* 1:1, a constellation of important interpretive tropes has emerged, a constellation essentially similar to what we discovered in the Targum to the Song. Both texts consistently, but in multiple ways, interpret the first verse of the Song in light of the exodus, Sinai (and the Torah associated with it), and the temple. As we have noted above, this is because by the late Second Temple period, the Song came to be understood to refer to the origins of the relationship between Israel and its God that began with the exodus, was solidified at Sinai, and maintained through the temple. Furthermore, note the strong association in tradition of Solomon with the temple, Torah (as author of three books in the Bible), and the Song of Songs. We have suggested how the interpreters play off of the language of the Song and associate its aesthetic beauty with its sacrality. All of these interpretive phenomena continue in the interpretation of verse 2.

1:2

The interpretation of verse 2 begins in chapter 12 of the midrash to the Song. Immediately we are presented with many of the textual associations we have outlined above. Recall the second verse, "Let him kiss me with the kisses of his mouth, For your love is better than wine." In explaining the verse, Rabbi Hinena says, "This was said at the Reed Sea." He supports this claim by citing Songs 1:9, which compares the beauty of the woman to the horses of Pharaoh. Hinena associates this imagery with that of the Egyptians pursuing the Israelites through the Reed Sea. The interpretation following Hinena's differs by suggesting that verse 2 was stated at Sinai. To prove this, Rabbi Yuda cites Ps 68:26, which reads, "The singers go before, the players after." The immediate reason for citing this passage depends on the similarity between the Hebrew words *singers* in Ps 68 and *songs* in the title to the Song (*sharim* versus *shirim* respectively). But, as usual, the larger context of the verse cited in Ps 68 informs Yuda's hermeneutic. Psalm 68:25 refers to "processions to the sanctuary"; the sanctuary (*qodesh*), by now, is a familiar interpretive lens for understanding the Song. Recall that the Song of the Sea in Exod 15 concludes with the imagery of God bringing his people to his mountain and sanctuary (*miqdash*—from the same root [*q-d-sh*] as *qodesh*). Moreover, the last third of Ps 68:26 mentions the "girls who play the tambourine," which includes the noun found in Song 1:3: "Therefore all the girls love you" (AT). Yuda likely sees in this constellation of words and imagery, a mutually illuminating resonance among Exod 15, Ps 68, and the Song; the significance of which is the notion that the second verse of the Song must have been declared at Sinai. The imagery and language of Ps 68 is highly reminiscent of Exod 15 where Miriam and a number of other women dance and sing the first verse of the Song of the Sea. All of this points to the fact that the interpreters read Song 1:2, Ps 68, and the Song of the Sea in such a way that all three illumine one another. Of course, the assumption here is that all three texts represent songs of which the Song of Songs is the best. Also, the associations implied between Ps 68 and Exod 15 reemphasize the connections between the Song of Songs, the exodus, and God's sanctuary.

Just a couple of interpretations after Yuda's, the midrash claims:

> Rabbi Meir says, "(Verse two) was said at the Tent of meeting" and he explains it from the following verse, "Arise, O north wind—come, O south, blow upon my garden and scatter its spices, Let my love come to his garden, and eat its lush fruit" (Song 4:16). "Arise, O north wind" refers to the burnt offering, which is slaughtered to the north (of the tent). "Come, O south" refers to the peace offerings slaughtered to its south. "Blow upon my garden" refers to the tent of meeting. "Scatter its spices" refers to the smoking incense. "Let my love come to his garden" refers to God's presence. "And eat its lush fruit" refers to the offerings.

Immediately following this interpretation, another repeats it nearly verbatim with the exception that it says the garden refers to the temple proper rather than the tent of meeting. This additional interpretation is superfluous to the degree that for most of biblical and Jewish tradition the tent of meeting and the temple were interchangeable. In fact, the case can be made that the tent of meeting is merely a biblical retrojection of the temple *in illo tempore*, the "golden age" prior to the building of the first temple. At any rate, the association of the second verse of the Song with the temple relies on an interpretive tack we have encountered repeatedly. In this instance, the imagery on which the interpreters rely suggests to them the sensuous activities associated with the temple. By associating these activities with its first few verses, the interpreters infer from the Song the divine delight in the sounds, smells, and tastes associated with both the Song and the temple sacrificial cult. The interpreters do not see this association only in its first few verses but in the whole of the Song. Indeed, immediately after the interpretation we have just considered, chapter 12 of the midrash suggests that Song 3:9-10 also refers to the temple. While this phenomenon may seem strange to the modern reader, it makes perfect sense in the context of the era following the destruction of the Second Temple in 70 C.E. In many ways, the rabbis view the Song as an attempt to capture in words the intimacy between Israel and God that was disrupted with the destruction of the temple. It was the temple that provided the traditional means of understanding God's nearness. In the absence of the temple, the rabbis desperately seek that intimacy in the words that remained. The Song was an excellent locus for that search, especially in the context of its resonance with the rest of Scripture. In the rabbinic mind, the reading of the Song becomes a way to revivify the richly sensuous practice that once filled the temple precincts. It is as if in reading and appreciating the sonal quality of the Song, they animate all of the activities and sensuous pleasures that marked God's association with Israel through the temple.

In an interpretive move that we have seen above, *Song Rab.* 13 associates the words of the Song with the Torah. The "kisses of his mouth" are here associated with a number of facets of the Torah. Rabbi Yohanan associates the kiss with an angel who was responsible for taking the "word of the Holy one, blessed be He" to all the Israelites with the goal of seeing who would accept (*meqabbel*) them. Another interpretation suggests that it was the word of God itself that made the rounds with the same goal. Finally, Rabbi Joshua ben Levi, playing off of the double occurrence of the root for "kiss" in verse 2 of the Song, suggests that there were two words that God spoke directly to Israel. These two "words" come from what is commonly referred to as the Ten Commandments but more properly is called the Decalogue. According to Rabbi Joshua ben Levi, the two words are the preamble (Exod 20:2) and the first commandment (Exod 20:3) of the Decalogue. The idea is that Israel heard these two verses directly from God rather than from Moses. The notion embedded in all of the interpretations from chapter 13 is that the imagery suggested the "kisses of his mouth" refers to the intimacy of God's relations with his people. In particular, that intimacy is consistently associated with the mouth of God from whom Israel has received his word or kisses. Again, this interpretation strongly associates the sensual pleasures of the Song with its verbal aesthetic and, in turn, associates that aesthetic with the beautiful words of the Torah.

Song of Songs Rabbah 14 also emphasizes the intimacy of God's relations with Israel, but does so by means of an analogy to the marriage between a king and the daughter of good and noble parents. Rabbi Yohanan uses this analogy to explain how it is that Israel spoke verse 2 of the Song on their ascent of Mount Sinai. Central to his explanation is the notion that a personified Israel, like the girl in Yohanan's parable, cannot accept that she is worthy of the king's affection. Suspecting that the messenger who brings the news might be unreliable, the girl requests that she hear it directly from the king's mouth. The midrash goes on to explain the characters in the parable: the king is God, the messenger Moses, and the girl Israel. Of most interest in the midrash is the presumption of the marriage between Israel and God that was initiated at Sinai. Furthermore, the interpretation sees in the kisses of 1:2 of the Song a reference to the words (Torah) that were given by God there.

In *Song Rab.* 15–16 we see interpretations that continue to associate the "kisses of his mouth" with Sinai and the giving of the Torah. Of particular interest is chapter 16 where Rabbi Eliezer says the situation in verse 2 of the Song can be compared to a king who had a wine cellar (*martef shel yayyin*). After giving only a single cup to two guests, the king gives the entire cellar to his son. The midrash presumes that God provided some commandments to Adam (cf. Gen 2:16) and Noah (cf. Gen 9:4), but that he preserved the entire Torah for Israel. The attentive reader will note an important shift in the imagery here. Whereas we have consistently seen the relationship between God and Israel depicted in terms of marriage, in this midrash the operative model is that of father and son. As noted in discussions above, early Jewish exegesis is known for its rapid movement among models for understanding theological realities.

This phenomenon reminds us that it is dangerous to seek consistent or conceptually monolithic modes of interpretation in these midrashim. Nonetheless, the familiar categories of the theology of love, temple, and Torah, predominate.

Of most interest in chapter 16 is the use of the word *wine*. By invoking this word and related imagery the midrash associates the wine of the Song with the words of the Torah. In doing so, it once again allows the narratives of the giving of the Torah and the poetry of the Song to coalesce and thus illumine each other. The result, as we have seen before, is to suggest not only that the Song is about the receiving of the Torah but also that those narratives are informed by the sensuous pleasures described in the Song. The association of the wine with the Torah is especially appropriate given the other oral elements of the early part of the Song. The midrash seems to say that the Torah is sweeter than wine. Further, it seems also to connect the oral pleasure of the Torah to its hearing, puns we have seen made especially in interpretations of verse 3 of the Song. We have seen, over and again, that the midrash takes what appears to be a relatively restricted approach to a specific word or image in the Song. In reality, however, it often presumes far more subtle associations across local and even more distant parts of the Song. For the interpreters of the midrash, the Song as a whole consistently alludes to the intimacy of the bond between Israel and its God that began at Sinai and was maintained though the two central Jewish categories of thought, the Torah and the temple.

We next turn to *Song Rab.* 19 to reveal the ways in which its interpreters associate the Song with the Torah. The midrash begins by claiming that the last half of verse 2 of the Song ("for your love is better than wine") is an example of the numerous ways in which the words of the Torah are compared to water, wine, oil, honey, and milk. The midrash next contains an extended discussion of the ways in which the Torah is associated with water, in particular. This association is so central to rabbinic thought, and to the argument of this study, that we need to consider some of the details of the way in which it is made. The midrash immediately cites roughly the first quarter of Isa 55:1 to make its point: "O, all who thirst, come for water!" (AT). As we have had occasion to note before, midrash often cites only a portion of the passage it views as pertinent. Indeed, it seems that the interpreters must have in mind much of the entirety of Isa 55. Note that all of Isa 55:1 reads:

> O, all who thirst,
> come for water,
> and he who is without money,
> Come, buy grain and eat:
> Come, buy grain with no money,
> Wine and milk at no price. (AT)

Clearly, part of the reason this passage is cited is that it includes three of the five items on the list with which the midrash opens. But there are, as usual, many more reasons for citing this passage. Note that Isa 55 goes on to describe the way in which its audience can be sated: by listening (*shim‘u* [*shamoa‘*]) to God in verses 2 and 3 so that he can establish an everlasting covenant which is the legacy of David (vv. 2-3).[5] Moreover, in luxuriant imagery verses 9-13 describe how the word that comes from God's mouth (*devari ʾasher yetseʾ mippi*) is like the snow and rain that falls to earth and brings forth vegetation. Further, the word of God, like the rain, brings forth the trees of the field that shall stand as a testimony (*shem*) to God. Embedded in this passage are what the rabbis see as multiple connections with the Song of Songs. First, they associate the listening to the word of God with the hearing of the Song itself. Also, just as the "kisses of the mouth" are none other than the words of the Torah coming from God's mouth, so the word that comes from the mouth of God in Isa 55:11 is understood to be the Torah. More specifically, Isa 55 directly compares the word of God to the rain and snow that brings forth the verdancy of the earth. Finally, the interpreters, no doubt, see in the word for testimony (*shem*) an allusion not only to God's name but also to the puns in verse 3 of the Song that play off of the words *name* (*shem*) and *oil* (*shemen*), which, in turn, seem to suggest the word for hearing (*sh-m-‘*) as well. Of great interest is that the interpreters find a biblical passage that makes exactly the point that they presume: God's word is associated with water and its life-sustaining qualities. Hosea 2 and Sir 24 harmonize well with this presumption. Furthermore, the interpreters recognize in the Isaiah passage imagery that goes to the heart of their understanding of the Song; God's word, embodied in the Song itself, helps sustain the verdancy that is everywhere described in the Song. For the interpreters, one merely need to heed Isa 55 by listening to the Song (do not miss the wordplay with the first four verses of the Song), which in turn activates the richly fertile world it describes. Once again, the theologically subtle reading of the Song is embedded in the interpreter's response to its (especially verbal) aesthetic.

Song of Songs Rabbah 19 continues to make similar associations between the Song and other passages in the Hebrew Bible. In fact, it cites a total of twenty-eight places in the Hebrew Bible in order to sustain the observation that the Torah is compared to water, wine, oil, honey, and milk. We need not detail the interpretive logic of each of the citations. It is significant that the fluid imagery of the Song 1:1-4 is replicated in their citations. Furthermore, the midrash reveals a fundamental tenet of rabbinic Judaism, the association of the Torah with fluid imagery, especially that of water. More important for this stage of our argument, the midrash associates the life-sustaining quality of water and its fundamental role in maintaining fertility with similar qualities of the Torah. For the interpreters, the Song, especially verse 2, is about the word of God associated with the "kisses of his mouth" and his Torah that is "better than wine." The lush and sensual language and imagery of the Song are understood to be the speech act by which God has animated his world. The continuity with the theology of love traced in part 1 of this study is remarkable.

1:3

The discussion in *Song of Songs Rabbah* on 1:3 is relatively brief, but there are a couple of issues that merit consideration. In chapter 20, Rabbi Yannay says, "All the songs that the forefathers sang before you were fragrances, but as for us, 'oil poured out is your name.'" Of interest is the way many of the elements we have been discussing are understood in Yannay's interpretation. For him, while all the other songs that appear in the Hebrew Bible are fragrant, this song, the Song of Songs, is the real source of that fragrance. Yannay seems to suggest that while oil can give off marvelous fragrance, its aroma is always a secondary by-product of the real thing. For him, the Song of Songs is the oil itself poured out. Yannay associates the sound of the Song with the sounds of oil poured out, and in turn with the very sound of God's name. Among several things that make this interpretation of interest, three in particular are important for our argument. First, the interpretation, like many we have considered above, is remarkably attentive to verbal assonance of the Song. Again, it hears in the language of verse 3 the association between the name (*shem*) and the oil (*shemen*) and observes that its fragrance is the key quality brought out by the first third of the verse. The second important observation embedded in Yannay's interpretation is related to the first; it conflates the sensuousness of the sounds, smells, and tastes with God's presence and then presumes all of these are part of the aesthetic of the Song. For Yannay, all of the sensuous delights of the Song are testament to God's presence in the very words of the Song and, by extension, the Torah. This brings us to the third and final insight suggested by Yannay's interpretation: the implication that the recital of the Song of Songs activates in a meaningful way God's name and by association his presence. Yannay essentially says that the Song represents the divine presence.

In the remainder of the midrash's commentary on Song 1:3, found in *Song Rab.* 21–23, we find a number of variations on familiar themes. In chapter 21, Rabbi Aha, noting the plural in the phrase "the fragrance of your oils too (is better than wine)," suggests that there are two oils just as there are two Torahs. As in many of the interpretations we have already encountered, this one hears in very words and sounds of the Song references to the Torah. In chapter 22, the interpreters see in the final phrase of verse 3, "therefore all the girls love you," a reference to Egypt at the time of the exodus. The details of the connection are obscure, but the theme is familiar. The same is true of chapter 23 where Ps 68:25 is cited once again to explain the last phrase of verse 3. Recall that above (discussion of *Song Rab.* 12) we considered the imagery of Ps 68 that almost assuredly is understood as a reference to the Song of Miriam in Exod 15:20. The girls of the Song of Songs are associated with the musicians of Ps 68 who, in turn, are associated with Miriam and her female troop of singers and musicians.

1:4

Song of Songs Rabbah 24–34 of our midrash comprise its commentary on the fourth verse of the first chapter of the Song. Because much here is familiar we will make a quick survey of the material, slowing where the subtlety of interpretation requires extended explanation. Chapter 24 begins with Rabbi Meir relating the story of Israel when they stood at the foot of Sinai in order to receive the Torah. Rather than provide any particular verbal association between the Song and the account of Sinai, Rabbi Meir presumes that his audience is familiar with this interpretive trope. The remainder of his discussion comes no closer to making the connection between the Song and the events at Sinai. Evidently, Rabbi Meir and his audience were so familiar with the association of the Song with the exodus that he did not even need to make the connection explicit. This is a good example of the emergence of the kind of literary and cultural competence that informs much of rabbinic interpretation. They are so immersed in the tradition of reading the Song in light of the exodus and Sinai that they no longer have to make reference to the connections they see between them, many of which we have been outlining above.

Song of Songs Rabbah 25 treats the first three words of verse 4, which translate to "draw me after you, let us run!" Rabbis Yohanan and Joshua claim that this line makes reference to God's bringing of his people to the land of Israel after the exodus and wilderness wanderings. The allusion to the exodus is nothing new, but the language they use to refer to the land of Israel is the key to this interpretation. Both rabbis refer to Israel as "a dwelling place" (*mishkenuta'*). This Aramaic noun is actually a pun on the Hebrew imperative verb *moshkheni*, "draw me," that begins verse 4. The midrash goes on to make other puns on this verb with references to God's presence, the noun for which in Hebrew (*shekhinah*) comes from the same root (*sh-k-n*) as the noun for "dwelling place."

Reading the imperative as the plea of Israel for God to draw them to him is consistent with other interpretations that see in the Song a reference to the exodus. This set of midrashim add to that imagery an emphasis on the possession of the land of Israel and, in particular, the notion of God's presence in the land. We have suggested above that the rabbis perceive in the Song the presence of God in its language and aesthetic. In chapter 25, the rabbis are explicit in this kind of reading. They associate the verb "draw" with two similar sounding words (*dwelling* and *presence*) that each make just that point. Furthermore, the rabbis make another pun on this imperative when the midrash cites Exod 25:8 to explain it. Here, God commands Moses to build the tabernacle, his mobile dwelling place among the Israelites while they are in the wilderness. The Hebrew name for this dwelling place of God is *mishkan*, from the same root as the Aramaic "dwelling place" and the Hebrew noun for God's "presence." The rabbis are not only making wordplay with the Song but also with the language of the book of Exodus as well. Embedded in their interpretation is the assumption that the Song celebrates the "presence" (*shekhinah*) of God, begun at the exodus when he drew (*moshkheni*) Israel after him and allowed his presence (*shekhinah*) to dwell (*mishkan*) among them until they entered the land that would become his and their permanent dwelling place (*mishkenuta'*). Recall that the *mishkan* represents a mobile temple and, once again, we see that the interpretation focuses on the centrality of the exodus and temple in the rabbis' understanding of God's love for Israel. So, in the single imperative verb that begins verse 4, the rabbis see a hint of nearly the entire history of Israel's association with God, from its origins just after the exodus to the fixing of God's presence in the temple. Moreover, once again, the rabbis infer that the language of the Song not only hints at this history but that its very sound is echoed at those defining moments of their history. In this sense, it seems that the interpreters hear in the Song a kind of reanimation of their sacred history that they think is alluded to therein.

Song of Songs Rabbah 26–27 of the midrash on Song of Songs continue to treat the phrase "draw me after you, let us run." Both chapters view this verse in light of the exodus and each takes advantage of puns on the imperative verb *moshkheni* as well. Of most interest is a brief interpretation at the end of chapter 27 that sees in the phrase "draw me after you" a reference to the closeness of the bond between God and Israel. The interpreters cite Ps 63:9, which reads, "My soul clings after you" (AT). The phrase from the Psalm includes the same prepositional phrase, "after you," that is found in Song 1:4. The rabbis, in turn, understand both phrases ("draw me after you" and "my soul clings after you") in light of the Torah writ large. In particular, they see in the imperative verb the call to read Scripture, Mishnah, Talmud, Tosefta, and Aggadah. Furthermore, they see in the psalm's passage the acknowledgment that it is through these Scriptures that they maintain their association with God. More significantly, they rely on language in the psalm that implies that the relationship is one of marriage. As we have seen throughout our discussion of early Jewish interpretation, the Song, once again, is understood to use the metaphors for human love common to the theology of love to convey the intimacy of God's relationship to his people.

Song of Songs Rabbah 27–34 comprise the final commentary on Song 1:4. These chapters interpret verse 4 in light of the motifs that we have witnessed in discussions above. A few examples of the interpretive motifs suffice to make this clear. For instance, in *Song Rab.* 30, the interpreters explain the phrase "let us rejoice and delight in you." The midrash claims that Israel is identified with ten different words that describe its joy. Each of the instances the midrash cites are cases in which Israel is said to rejoice or take delight in the Lord. Clearly, this interpretation views the antecedent of "you" in the phrase "let us rejoice and delight in you" as God himself. This is to be expected given the interpretive stance that we have seen in all of the early Jewish material we have considered. One more example from the final eight chapters of the midrash is worth considering. In chapter 31, we are told that the phrase "we will rejoice and delight in you" can be compared to the case of a queen whose husband, sons, and sons-in-law went away. When told her sons and sons-in-law were returning, she said that her daughters-in-law and daughters could rejoice but that it made little difference to her. In contrast, when told that her husband was to return, the queen said that this is the occasion of great joy. The midrash goes on to claim that this story is like the age to come when prophets will announce the return of the king, and the queen (read "Israel") will rejoice. Again, not only is the relationship between Israel and God conceived as marriage, but the Song is understood to adumbrate future rejoicing when God returns to his temple in the world to come.

Summary of Early Jewish Interpretation

Having surveyed the Targum and Midrash Rabbah to the first four verses of the Song, we need to summarize our findings. We have seen how consistently the interpreters view the Song in light of three motifs in particular: the exodus, Torah, and temple. Over and again, these motifs form the lens by which the early Jewish interpreters view the Song, its motifs, language, and even its aesthetic. Each of these motifs is further understood to be an expression of the love of God for Israel. Of most interest is the centrality that the Torah and temple take in interpreting the Song of Songs. Our discussion in part 1 of this study was devoted to tracing the emergence in the late Second Temple period of these two basic motifs for understanding God's intimate connection to Israel. It is that conceptual history that provides the foundation for the Jewish interpretive edifice.

In addition to the consistently theological way in which the interpreters view the Song, we have argued that its very aesthetic lends itself to such a reading. In particular, the interpreters hear in the Song's beautiful aural quality an aesthetic that simultaneously evokes the temple and other parts of Scripture, including the Torah. It is their attentiveness to the specific language and imagery of the Song that makes early Jewish interpretation of the Song so compelling. In many ways, their interpretations can be seen as a response to the subtle self-referential quality of the Song itself. In fact, the early Jewish interpreters can be understood to extend these qualities of poetics, the composition of the Song, to its interpretation; they see in its sexual metaphors reference to the larger literary context of the Hebrew Bible.

In the next chapter, we consider Origen's commentary and sermon on the first four verses of chapter 1 of the Song. In doing so we accomplish several things. First, Origen interprets the Song in ways that are, *mutatis mutandis*, strikingly similar to the early Jewish interpretations. Indeed, Origen is considered the parent of Christian interpretation of the Song, which saw in it the love of Christ for the church or individual believer. Moreover, Origen seems to presume much the same attitude about the Song's aesthetic as we have seen in the Targum and midrash. Furthermore, just as Jewish interpretation sees in the Song the greatest moment of salvation in Jewish history (the exodus), so does Origen. We shall see, however, that for Origen that moment is not the exodus, but the Christian equivalent in Jesus' life, death, and resurrection. It remains, then, to consider Origen's understanding of the Song and its place in his theology of love.

CHAPTER SIX

ORIGEN'S HOMILY AND COMMENTARY TO SONG OF SONGS 1:1-4

As noted, Origen is credited with setting the agenda for nearly all of Christian interpretation of the Song that came after him.[1] Origen's commentary and homilies on the Song have not survived in the original Greek. We do have the Latin translations of the commentary by Rufinus and the homilies by Jerome.[2] The approach one takes in using these texts must differ from the use of the Hebrew and Aramaic texts considered above. This is true for a number of reasons. First, because we now have only a Latin translation, we cannot count on the close verbal comparisons that informed our understanding of the Jewish texts. In the process of translation, one can never be sure of the degree to which the Latin corresponds to Origen's Greek. Where Greek fragments have survived, it is clear our translators have felt free to be rather loose in their representation of Origen's original. Furthermore, it is difficult to determine when the translators are treating an issue related to the Latin text of the Song that they knew or if they are merely repeating Origen's analysis of the Greek. As a result of these factors, our analysis of Origen necessarily treats the more general issues of his approach to the Song and the categories by which he understands it, rather than concentrating on verbal specificity, which is lost to us through translation.

Analysis of Origen's treatment of the Song reveals that he shares with Jewish interpreters the assumption that it is about the love of God for his people. Indeed, we hear in Origen what seem to be echoes of Jewish tradition.[3] This is so much the case that the Jewish typology in which the Song came to be linked with Torah has its analogue in Origen in his association of the Song with Jesus as the Word. This goes far in explaining why the Song, understood as representative of Torah for Jews and the Word for Christians, became so treasured.

Origen's Prologue to His Commentary on Song of Songs 1:1-4

Origen's prologue to his commentary is divided into four parts; the first is titled "The Song of Songs, a Drama of Mystical Meaning"; the second, "The Theme of the Song of Songs"; the third, "The Place of the Song of Songs among the Works of Solomon"; and the fourth, "The Title 'Song of Songs.'" It is in the prologue that we get some sense of Origen's theological assumptions about the Song. Here we encounter his elaboration of the ways in which the Song is representative of the love of God for his people.

In the first part of his prologue, Origen addresses what he views as the original purpose of the Song. He claims that the Song is "a marriage-song, which Solomon wrote in the form of a drama and sang under the figure of the Bride, about to wed and burning with heavenly love towards her Bridegroom, who is the Word of God."[4] Clearly Origen accepts the authenticity of Solomon's authorship of the Song, as did Jewish interpreters. More important, the attentive reader likely recognizes in Origen's claim something familiar. Indeed, the association of the Song with the Word is dependent on the history of interpretation of Prov 8:22 that we have elaborated on in chapter 3 of this study. In order to fully understand Origen's insight, a brief review of that history is in order. Recall that in Prov 8:22 Wisdom says, "The LORD created me at the beginning of His course, / As the first of His works of old." The interpretive culture of Second Temple Judaism came to understand that Wisdom was created first and was something like a helpmate in the process of creation. We also outlined above the interpretation of Sirach (in ch. 24) in which he reflects that Wisdom came to be associated with Torah. Furthermore, recall that in Sirach, Wisdom/Torah were associated with fertility of the world in language that was remarkably resonant with the Song of Songs.

The tradition of interpretation of Wisdom's role in creation, carried on after Sirach, and two more historical snapshots help us understand Origen's perspective. In late Second Temple Judaism, in particular among Jews living under Greek authority, there was an effort to understand the relationship of the biblical tradition to Greek culture. Among the most famous minds to work on this project was Philo Judaeus of Alexandria (ca. 20 B.C.E.–50 C.E.). In part of his work, Philo attempts to understand the interpretive tradition of Prov 8 in categories of Greek thought. Key to this understanding was the association of Wisdom/Torah, which was the word of God after all, with the notion of the logos, Greek for "word."[5] Two texts in the Hebrew Bible were central in making this association. First, Gen 1 records that God created the world merely by speaking. Familiar to all is the sequence, "He said . . . and it was so." The second text that helps explain the linkage between Torah and logos is found in Ps 33:6 where we read, "By the word [*davar*] of YHWH the heavens were made, by the breath of his mouth [*pihu*], all their Host" (AT).[6] The Greek translation of the Hebrew for *word* (*davar*) was, of course, *logos*. In Philo's conception, it was the logos that was God's helpmate from the beginning of creation. Finally, the Gospel of John represents something of the same interpretive tradition in identifying Jesus as the Word. As John 1:1 has it, "In the beginning was the Word, and the Word was with God, and the Word was God" (NRSV).

That Origen understands the Song to be about the deep love of the church or individual believer for the Word is clearly indebted to the Jewish tradition of interpretation of Prov 8, Sirach, and the larger association of the Song with the garden of Eden and the origins of God's relationship to his people. When Origen invokes the notion that the Song is about the passion for the Word, he is part of a tradition that had echoed throughout late Second Temple Judaism, and that associated the Word with the Torah/Wisdom (that is to say, with Scripture). Like his Jewish predecessors, Origen seems to suggest that the Word, understood as this divine counterpart to God and present from the earliest creation, is exquisitely sensual and the highest manifestation of the divine. Furthermore, Jewish readers and Origen see the Song as a manifestation of that divine entity and representative of God's presence. In addition, they likely presume the connection of the Song to the Wisdom tradition and, therefore, understand the Song to represent an account of the saving role Wisdom plays in Wis 10:1–11:4. Here, in the first part of this prologue, Origen tips his hat, perhaps unwittingly, to the history of interpretation that held the Song and its language in such high esteem. More to the point, like his Jewish contemporaries, Origen sees the Song through the lens of Sirach where, we have argued, the Song is understood to be part of the Wisdom tradition and a description of the lush world that Wisdom produces. The final point we wish to highlight from the first part of the prologue is Origen's explicit reference to the Jewish tradition of allowing only mature adults to read the Song. This is significant because Origen clearly knew Jewish tradition relating to the Song. As we shall see below, at points in his interpretation Origen seems self-consciously to use and adapt Jewish interpretive tradition for the purpose of revealing the superiority of Christianity.

The second part of Origen's prologue is titled "The Theme of the Song of Songs." Here, he stresses that in the Bible the terms for *love* (charity and passion) refer to a love that finds its origin in God himself. While Scripture usually avoids the use of the term *passion*, Origen argues, it does occasionally appear when there can be no confusion about the object of desire. For example, he cites Prov 4:6, 8 and Wis 8:2 where the term *passion (eros)* is used in reference to the love of wisdom. This all comes in the context of Origen's insistence that the appropriate form of passion in humans is affection for the Word of God, which is none other than Jesus. As Origen puts it:

> Having clearly beheld the beauty and fairness of the Word of God, it [the soul] falls deeply in love with His loveliness and receives from the Word Himself a certain dart and wound of love. For this Word *is the image* and splendour *of the invisible God, the Firstborn of all creation, in whom were all things created that are in heaven and on earth, seen and unseen alike.*[7]

The italicized part of the previous quote comes from Col 1:15-16. It, like Origen, is dependent on the history of interpretation of Prov 8:22 and especially Sir 24. More important is that once again we see the reinforcement of the notion that the passion described in the Song is first for the Word of God, understood as Jesus. Secondarily, this passion is elicited by the very nature of the word of Scripture of which the Song is a part.

The third part of the prologue treats the place of the Song of Songs within the works ascribed to Solomon. Origen asks why the three books so ascribed appear in the following order: Proverbs, Ecclesiastes

(Qohelet), and Song of Songs. His answer is that the Greeks actually borrowed their division of human knowledge into moral, natural, and "inspective" from the order of Solomon's books in the Bible. The anachronism and assumption of cultural superiority here need not detain us, of most import is that for Origen the Song comes last because it represents the last of the three divisions of human understanding. In this scheme, the Song represents the culmination of learning of moral and natural teaching to be found in Proverbs and Qohelet respectively. It is only after mastery of those divisions of learning that one comes to see clearly "behind" the apparent reality. Here Origen makes the case, based on his understanding of the Greek curriculum, for the allegorical meaning of the Song. It is not meant to be read on the moral or "natural" level but, rather, on the level of allegory wherein the true meaning is theological—about *"the things that are not seen, and that are eternal."* [8]

In the fourth part of his prologue, Origen addresses issues relating to the title of the Song of Songs. Because his discussion is essentially commentary on verse 1 of the Song, we shall consider this material in conjunction with our analysis of his homily to Song of Songs 1:1 below.

To summarize: in the prologue Origen comes closest to elaborating the assumptions that inform his reading of the Song. As we have seen, he makes the case for an allegorical reading of the text that sees beyond the merely human trappings of love to expose the great passion that the Church or individual ought to have for God. Further, he argues that this passion is presented in the form of a drama in which the church or individual soul longs for its lover, the Word. Through appeals to what he knows as Scripture, Origen makes explicit the association of the Word with Jesus. This association is important in two respects. First, Origen's equivalent of the Jewish tradition of Torah, the Word, presumes the theology of love outlined in part 1 of this study and resonates remarkably with his Jewish contemporaries. Second, and perhaps less obvious, is that the temple, as part of the theology of love, is implicit in his reading as well. Jesus can be understood to be a transformation of the ancient Israelite and Jewish rites associated with the temple. Whereas in the Hebrew Bible and Jewish tradition the atonement for and cleansing from sin came through sacrificial rites associated with the temple (the tabernacle in the Pentateuch being a microcosm of the temple), Jesus replaces those rites in his death as sacrifice in early Christian thought. While the attitude toward the temple in the New Testament is ambiguous, the fact that Jesus supplants the rites associated with it suggests that those rites were as integral to early Christianity as they were to the Second Temple Judaism from which it arose. More to the point, like Jewish interpretation before him (albeit substantially reformulated), Origen sees the passionate love of God's people for the Torah (Jesus as the Word) and temple (Jesus the Redeemer) as the subject of the Song. Origen's understanding of the significance of the Song in terms of Word and temple make him part of a tradition of the theology of love that is the subject of this book.

Just two more significant elements of Origen's prologue need detain us. First, as noted above, like his Jewish predecessors, Origen presumes not only the sacral nature of the Song itself but also of the language in which it is expressed; the Word is, after all, Jesus himself. Second, Origen reads the Song in light of other Scripture (again as in Jewish interpretation). Of course this includes both the New and Old Testaments. This habit of reading the Song in light of other Scripture is equally clear in his actual commentary and homilies on the Song, to which we now turn.

Origen's commentary and homily on the first four verses of the Song are profitably considered together. In the following, we shall consider first his commentary to each verse and then turn to his sermon on the same verse. Complicating our discussion is that the version of the Bible from which Origen worked has different versification from the Hebrew. In the following we will use the Hebrew versification but at times, because Origen discusses the material in slightly different segments, we will need to follow his argument even when it crosses verse distinctions in the Hebrew.

1:1

Origen's commentary on the first verse of the Song appears as the fourth part of his prologue but is best considered here as part of his verse-by-verse commentary. Origen, like his Jewish counterparts, understands the title of the Song of Songs to suggest that it is the best among many songs. Unlike his Jewish contemporaries, however, Origen's list of songs comprises the "top seven" rather than "top ten." James Kugel has pointed out that Origen's list includes five of the ten songs that appear in a list in the Mekilta de-Rabbi Ishmael.[9] Unfortunately, we cannot be sure Origen's list is indebted to the rabbinic listing of the songs. Because he repeats this discussion in his homily, we take it up below.

Origen next asks why the Song is attributed to Solomon with no reference, as in Proverbs and Qohelet, to his relationship to David and his role as king. Origen claims that it is because as a cipher for Jesus, Solomon has attained to such perfection that mundane categories no longer apply. As Origen puts it, "He [Jesus] has become as the Lord."[10] Origen's association of Solomon with Jesus is based on the etymology of Solomon's name, which is from the Hebrew root having to do with peace. For Origen, the connection is obvious since Jesus is, for him and his Christian contemporaries, the Prince of Peace.

Finally, Origen argues against a tradition that reads the first verse to mean that the Song is the best among Solomon's various songs. Origen notes that this understanding is based on 1 Kgs 5:12 where we are told that Solomon composed three thousand parables and one thousand and five songs.[11] This understanding, however, is mistaken according to Origen. The title of the Song merely means that the Song is the best there is and that it is by Solomon. It appears that because Origen ascribed divine status to the Song, he thought it inappropriate to consider it among a vast number of other songs composed by Solomon.

In his homily, Origen, addressing the meaning of the name "Song of Songs," sounds much like his Jewish contemporaries and echoes Rabbi Aqiba. Origen notes that Moses himself suggested "that some places are not merely holy, but *holy of holies*, and that certain days are not sabbaths simply, but are sabbaths of sabbaths: so now we are taught further by the pen of Solomon that there are songs which are not merely songs, but SONGS OF SONGS" (ACW 266). Origen goes on to claim that much is required of the man who enters the holy of holies, just as of one who would understand the Song of Songs. Implicit here are a number of associations. Again we see the resort to Hebrew grammar to explain the superlative. Of interest, and perhaps only because it is the best-known example, Origin, like Aqiba, cites the phrase "holy of holies." Origin likely presumes at some deep level the association of the temple and its attendant rites and ablutions with Jesus. While this must remain conjecture, it is clear that Origin associates the love of the Word (Jesus) with the holy of holies, the most sacred precinct in the temple complex.

Origen continues his discussion of the title in more mundane terms. As in the prologue to his commentary, here in his sermon he claims the Song is the seventh of a number of songs found in the Hebrew Bible. The first song is the one that Moses and the Israelites sang just after crossing the Reed Sea in Exod 15. Like his Jewish contemporaries, Origen views the Song of Songs, the best of all songs in the Hebrew Bible, in light of the Song of the Sea, which marked the beginning of the redemption of the Israelite people. Once again, it is highly likely that Origen sees in the Song of Songs (and its association with Jesus) the culmination of the acts of God's redemption that started so long ago with the exodus.

Origen goes on to speculate on the actors who recite the lines of the Song. Of significance, he proposes that the main male character or bridegroom is Christ and the bride is the church *"without spot or wrinkle*, of whom it is written: *that He might present her to Himself a glorious Church, not having spot or wrinkle or any such thing, but that she might be holy and without blemish."*[12] By citing Eph 5:27, Origen presumes the self-referential quality of Scripture. In his mind, Ephesians is treating exactly the same issue that is the subject of the Song—Christ as bridegroom, and the church or individual Christian as the bride. The last four words of the quote from Ephesians deserve some attention. "Holy and without blemish" is a phrase generally associated in the Hebrew Bible with appropriate sacrifice that can be offered at the temple or tabernacle. While here it refers to the church rather than Christ, it is worth noting that the phrase finds its logical and ritual home in the temple and in the rite of sacrifice. Once again, Scripture, and those who know it well, often make such associations even when they seem logically reversed. At any rate, the quote from Ephesians comes from a section that is actually part of the development of the theology of love that is the topic of the present work.

1:2

Origen turns next to the first half of verse 2, "Let him kiss me with the kisses of his mouth." While on the surface the bride who longs for her groom speaks this, the real supplicant, according to Origen, is the church. As he puts it:

> The Church as a corporate personality . . . speaks and says: "'I am sated with the gifts which I received as betrothal presents or as dowry before my marriage. For of old, while I was being prepared for my wedding with the King's Son and the Firstborn of all creation, His holy angels put themselves at my service and ministered to me, bringing me the Law as a betrothal gift; for *the Law*, it is said, *was ordained by angels in the hand of a mediator*. The prophets also ministered to me."[13]

Origen goes on to explain that the church was informed of the coming of the Christ (the groom) through the words of the prophet who inflamed the bride with passionate expectation. Impatient with the wait, the bride exclaims:

> "I pour out my petition to Thee, the Father of my Spouse, beseeching thee to have compassion at last upon my love, and to send Him, that He may now no longer speak to me only by His servants the angels and the prophets, but may come Himself, directly, and kiss me with the kisses of His mouth—that is to say, may pour the words of His mouth into mine, that I may hear Him speak Himself, and see Him teaching. The kisses are Christ's, which He bestowed on His Church when at His coming, . . . being the words of faith and love and peace, according to the promise of Isaias who, when sent beforehand to the Bride, has said: *'Not a messenger, nor an angel, but the Lord Himself shall save us.'* " [14]

Each of the two quotes above ends in a citation of Scripture that helps put in perspective Origen's understanding of the Song. The first seems to be a reference to Gal 3:19, the second to Isa 33:22. Like most Christians, Origen sees in each of these citations reference to the events of which the Song speaks only elliptically. The Hebrew Bible and the New Testament (the former proleptically and the latter after the fact), attest to the reality that the prophets were merely tantalizing the church with what was to come to full fruition in Christ.[15] That the Song speaks of these same hopes in such beautifully elliptical language shows all the more how in touch it is with these exquisite realities. For Origen, it is when the believer or church receives the Word of God, not through intermediaries but, as it were, mouth to mouth, that the proper and intimate relationship is established between God and humans.

In his sermon on the first half of verse 2, Origen is brief. Much like his commentary, he suggests that the bride ask God to send his Son, her groom, that she may kiss him:

> "How long is my Bridegroom going to send me kisses by Moses and kisses by the prophets? It is His own mouth that I desire now to touch; let Him come, let Him come down Himself!" So she beseeches the Bridegroom's Father saying: "Let him kiss me with the kisses of His mouth." (ACW 269)

While this is reminiscent of the material in his commentary, one thing in particular deserves attention. Origen, knowingly or not, picks up on the rabbinic tradition of Moses' face-to-face meeting with God. As in his commentary, Origen imagines the bride to have tired of the kisses by proxy and now desires the face-to-face meeting for which she has waited so long. In fact, as the quote above from his commentary suggests, the bride awaits the time that Christ will "pour the words of His mouth" into hers (ACW 60). Like Jewish interpreters, Origen seems to pick up and elaborate on the fluid imagery of the Song itself. It is highly likely that he has in mind the oral pleasure of kissing in the first instance and, secondarily, the notion of the pouring out of ointments associated with Jesus' name in verse 3.

Most significant in Origen's understanding of verse 2 is his presumption of the obsolescence of the Jewish tradition and, in particular, the Hebrew Bible. In his interpretation, the bride awaits the real thing, the kisses of the Word itself rather than what Origen imagines are its second-rank predecessors. We might interpret this emphasis on the direct and unmediated communication as analogous to the rabbinic doctrine of the two Torahs. For early rabbinic interpretation, the pair, written and oral Torah, did have the force of the distinction between exoteric versus esoteric. While this may be at least part of Origen's perception, he likely joins much of early Christianity in asserting its superiority over Judaism. Clearly, it is ironic that Origen puts so much value on the Song of Songs, a part of his Old Testament, in making the case for the superiority of the New. He sounds like much of early Christianity in attempting to claim legitimacy from the Jewish tradition while, simultaneously, undercutting it. Moreover, that Origen understands the kisses of verse 2 to refer to a face-to-face meeting with God may suggest that he was aware of the Jewish tradition that understood this verse to refer to Moses' face-to-face encounter. To the degree that he does so, there is deep irony in Origen's turning this encounter into a repudiation of the very law that Jews understood was communicated in that encounter.

Origen translates the second half of verse 2 differently from us. Rather than, "For your love is better than wine," he reads, "Your breasts are better than wine." Still understood to come from the bride, this seems like an odd reading. In fact, however, it is representative of the LXX and the Latin translation from which Origen's translators worked, and is justifiable based on the Hebrew. The Hebrew root we have translated as *love* (*d-w-d*) can also be translated "breast," and some translations opt for the latter meaning. More to the point, what could the bride mean by drawing attention to the breasts of Christ? Origen argues that this represents the point at which the groom has arrived and the bride is taken aback by his beauty and fragrance. Clearly, Origen addresses the transition from third-person reference in the first half of the verse to the second person in the second half of verses 2 and 3. The deeper meaning, according to Origen, is that the breast represents the heart or bosom. He then cites several New Testament passages that make reference to Christ's chest and concludes, "Indeed I think the term 'the bosom of Christ' is not unfitting, if it be taken as denoting the place of holy teachings."[16] In fact, later on Origen notes that "in certain versions we find written FOR THY SAY-INGS ARE BETTER THAN WINE, where we read 'For Thy breasts are better than wine.' "[17] The question then arises, what does the wine represent? Origen makes the case, based on a number of scriptural references, that wine is essentially the teaching of the Hebrew Bible, in particular the Law and the Prophets.[18] Having made the case earlier that the bride first longs for the kisses of her groom rather than settle for the "kisses" of the Law and Prophets, Origen brings home the argument by claiming that the bride recognizes in Christ, her groom, beauty and teaching more worthy than those former dispensations. Once again, Origen finds a way to dismiss Jewish readings of the Song.

In his sermon on the second half of verse 2, Origen repeats, albeit more vaguely, the case that the wine represents the Law and Prophets but adds to his explanation by claiming that by association with Christ the believer (bride) becomes equally fragrant. There follows a discussion of the putrid smell of sin and the cleansing of Christ.[19] In a brief digression, for which he apologizes, Origen goes on to claim that through association with Christ and his teaching (remember the fragrance is thought to be his teaching) one gains a "spiritual" desire and love as opposed to those of the "flesh."[20]

1:3-4

Origen's version of verses 3 and 4 differs so much from the Hebrew that it is difficult to divide his discussion according to the latter. In order to do justice to his thought, we follow his divisions of verses 3 and 4, his version of which follows:

> The fragrance of Thine ointments is above all spices. . .
> [*Thy name is as ointment emptied out. Therefore have the*
> *maidens loved Thee, have they drawn thee. We will run after*

Thee into the fragrance of Thine ointments.] . . . The King hath brought me into His chamber. Let us rejoice and be glad in Thee. We will love Thy breasts more than wine. Equity hath loved Thee."[21]

A quick glance at this translation reveals a number of differences from the Hebrew. These shall be taken up as they occur. First, verse 3 actually completes the thought of the second half of verse 2, the reading of which should be something like, "For your love is better than wine, the fragrance of your oils too." Origen's translation has decided to take the first part of verse 3 as separate from the end of verse 2. More to the point, Origen tells his audience that the fragrant ointments are a reference to Christ's anointing and that the spices to which these ointments are compared, once again, represent the Law in the Hebrew Bible. Lest one think that the Law or Hebrew Bible are meant by the ointments, Origen goes to great length to establish that they are, indeed, associated with Christ. Among his many proofs, the following is both typical and, to him, most convincing: "God anointed Him [Christ] who *loved justice and hated iniquity*. For *therefore*, Scripture says, *hath the Lord His God anointed Him with the oil of gladness above His fellows*."[22] By making reference to Gal 5:22 and Ps 45:8, Origen suggests that both the New Testament and the Hebrew Bible recognized the superiority of the anointing of Jesus. Further, Origen implies that 1:3 of the Song is an allusion to this same reality. Moreover, the attentive reader my have noticed that Origen, like the Targum, associates the ointment or oil of verse 3 with the notion of the Messiah. Of course, the Targumist's understanding of the messiah would be at odds with Origen's, but in both instances the association of the Song with the Messiah expresses the hope of renewed intimacy with God, and, ultimately, redemption.

In his commentary and sermon Origen next turns to the passage bracketed above that represents part of verse 3 and 4 in the Hebrew.[23] The Hebrew in this passage is closer to the following, "Oil poured out is your name, therefore all the girls love you. Draw me after you, let us run." Note that verse 3 is roughly the same as the Hebrew but that Origen's represents a significantly expanded first part of verse 4. Origen explains that the "ointments poured out" represent the spreading of the word and name of Christ throughout the world; an anointing of the world, if you will.[24] The purpose of this "good news," claims Origen, is that "these maiden souls at the beginning of their progress might not only love Him, but might draw Him to themselves."[25] By so reading, Origen changes the request by the young woman to be drawn after her lover to a declarative in which the maidens, who represent Christians, souls, and the church writ large, draw Christ toward them.[26] In Origen's mind, the sweet fragrance and beauty of Christ are so compelling that anyone would draw him near. Also, as the last part of his version has it, they would run after him.

Next, Origen suggests that it is not merely the fragrance of Christ that attracts. He makes his point in the form of a question: "What, do you think, will they do when the Word of God takes possession of their hearing, their sight, their touch, and their taste as well, and offers excellences from Himself that match each single sense according to its nature and capacity, . . . ?" Origen goes on to invoke the mana from heaven in exodus and other biblical examples where food is associated with God.[27] He concludes this line of thought by saying that the mature Christian "will be delighted by the Word of God in all his senses."[28] Here, Origen seems tacitly to acknowledge that the Song itself invokes all the senses. For Origen, the fullness of the experience of Christ is represented by the invocation of all the senses in the Song. We saw above that Jewish interpreters used the language of all the senses in describing the events of the Song (exodus) but that they were not as explicit in associating them with God.

In his concluding remarks on the issue of the senses, Origen emphasizes that one needs to understand that this is spiritual and referential rather than physical language. He insists that only the mature and sincere Christian is capable of this deeper and true understanding of the Song.

In the last section of his commentary, Origen addresses the passage "The King hath brought me into His chamber. Let us rejoice and be glad in Thee. We will love Thy breasts more than wine. Equity hath loved Thee" (ACW 84). He explains that in bringing his bride, the faithful believer or church, into his chamber, Christ the groom and king is revealing his "own secret and mysterious mind."[29] In addition, when all the maidens say, "Let us rejoice," they are hoping that they too might be privy to the wonders of Christ's mind. Furthermore, when the maidens exclaim that they "will love thy breasts more than wine," they look forward to the time when, once allowed access to Christ's mind, they too can enjoy fully his teaching and presence. Finally, in the last sentence of the quote above, Origen claims that the maidens confess their own iniquity, and resultant distance from Christ, by admitting that equity or purity is capable of "loving [his] breasts more than wine" currently.[30] As he puts it in his sermon, whereas the bride, Equity, now fully understands and loves Christ's teaching, one day the maidens will as well.[31]

Summary of Origen's Reading of the Song

Clearly, Origen presumes the theology of love in his reading of the Song of Songs. This is especially clear in his dependence on the history of interpretation of Prov 8 and the association of the Song with Jesus as the Word. As a late Second Temple variation on the notion of Wisdom that was eternal, the Word represents for Origen much the same thing that Torah does for his Jewish contemporaries. As we saw in the Jewish interpretation, so for Origen; the sensual nature of the Song was understood to be integrally linked to the fecund world that Wisdom/Torah/Word had a hand in creating at the origin of God's work.

That Origen sees in the Song such a strong association with Jesus suggests his presumption of the two pillars of the theology of love that we have described in part 1 of this study. Clearly, Jesus as the Word is understood to be not just a replacement for Torah, but its final and correct dispensation. So wonderful is the Word that it renders obsolete what Origen and other Christians understood to be the former dispensation. Furthermore, to the degree that Origen understands Jesus to represent the ultimate and final sacrifice, he also views the Song in imagery associated with the temple.

Origen joins Jewish interpretation in understanding the Song of Songs in categories that are most at home in the theology of love that we have discussed in this study. It is to the conclusions that we can draw from this discussion that we must now turn.

CHAPTER SEVEN

CONCLUSION

We began this study with the assertion that the Song of Songs made it into the Hebrew Bible because it was understood to be part of the theology of love in the Hebrew Bible. Indeed, we now recognize that for early interpreters the Song likely represented the finest and most articulate formulation of that theology. It is time to sort out the varying influences that led to the inclusion of the Song in the Hebrew canon.

We first considered the prophetic formulation of the theology of love in its marriage/adultery motif. Clearly, the most important presumption on the part of the prophets is that Israel and YHWH are married. We also have seen that while the prophets are in the midst of crises, they continually wax nostalgic in remembering the early days of the relationship. Hosea movingly refers to those halcyon days in 2:17 when he says, "There she shall respond as in the days of her youth, / When she came up from the land of Egypt." Hosea, like the tradition of interpretation of the Song, sees in the exodus and wilderness wanderings the origins of this promising love affair. Jeremiah shares this understanding: "I accounted to your favor / The devotion of your youth, / Your love as a bride— / How you followed Me in the wilderness, / In a land not sown" (2:2). Ezekiel 16 records a similarly nostalgic account of the early days of the relationship if not in terms explicitly resonant with the exodus. He does, however, refer to the covenant when he says, "I spread My robe over you and covered your nakedness, and I entered into a covenant with you" (16:8).

Each of the prophets we have considered also depicts the early stage of the marriage, and the subsequent years of marital bliss, in the language of fertility and abundance. It is only with acts of infidelity that this abundance begins to fade. Depicted as adultery, the prophets take aim on Israel's apostasy. In terms most personal, they articulate what they perceive to be God's great disappointment and heartbreak. As cuckold, YHWH is not silent. He rages at his spouse and, in quite human terms, threatens to withhold the favors that come from him. Yet, things can be made better if only Israel will wake up and return to the love of her youth. The theology of love and early interpretation of the Song merely express the hope that such a reconciliation is imminent.

Several salient issues arise in the prophetic material that are crucial to elaborating the development of the theology of love and, as a consequence, the impetus to include the Song of Songs in the Hebrew Bible. First is, again, the presumption of the fertile and rich benefits of this marriage. The idealized descriptions of the early days are central to the prophetic call to return. In this sense, one can understand how the biblical tradition might read the Song of Songs as an extended description of what are relatively brief accounts in the Prophets. In the Song they could and did read the detailed account of the wonders of the early days. Aiding in this reading is, no doubt, that the Song could also be read as a description of another protological moment—the days in the garden of Eden. Understood in such light, as a dual reference to the origins of life and the origins of the covenant community, the Song could take pride of place as a recollection of days gone by. Strengthening the Song's association with the garden of Eden was Sirach chapter 24 in which his description of the role of Wisdom/Torah at creation is in language so resonant with the Song. Reading the Song in light of Eden and the honeymoon of the exodus was especially important in the late Second Temple period when doubts about God's presence and fidelity were hard to avoid.

Another important issue that our discussion of the prophets brings out is one that seems obscure at first; it is what I have labeled the nakedness-exposed motif. While Hosea alludes to it first, it seems to crystallize in language and imagery in Jer 13. Jeremiah's formulation seems to influence subsequent use of the motif, and we saw that Ezekiel and Nahum employ language and imagery that is so similar it is hard to avoid the impression that there is a genetic relationship among all three. Significant in this traditionary process is that Nahum applies the nakedness-exposed motif in such a novel way. Recall that Ezek 16:8 refers to the covering of nakedness as integral to the founding of the covenant. One can immediately see that in most of the prophets the exposing of nakedness, implying vulnerability, is symbolic of the breaking of the covenant. Nahum's application of the motif to Nineveh is as creative as it is incongruous.[1] This may simply suggest how adaptable biblical motifs are, but the implications are important. If Nineveh is depicted as a wanton woman and seductress, does it imply that Israel, in the prophetic tradition as one who consorts with foreigners, is now conceived of as the male partner? An answer to this question is impossible, but as we saw in our discussion of the Wisdom material, especially in Prov 5 and Sirach, just such a reversal of gender does take place.

Equally important in the evolution of the nakedness-exposed motif is that we see allusions to it in Lam 1:10 where the language of unclean skirts appears. It would appear that Lam 1 has picked up on the last important issue we need to discuss in reference to the prophetic marriage/adultery motif: the association of sexual defilement with the cult and tabernacle/temple.

Each of the prophets who employ the marriage/adultery motif direct their complaints at apostasy. In Hosea this apostasy comprises worship of Baal. This would comprise not merely devotion but also sacrifice to an alien god. Because the prophets perceive Israel's relationship to YHWH to be monogamous, any attention paid to another is unacceptable. Jeremiah also takes aim on devotion to Baal in 2:8 where he says, "The prophets prophesied by Baal," but seems to extend the indictment to unsavory alliances with Egypt and Assyria. In 13:10, Jeremiah accuses Judah and Jerusalem of following other Gods. Ezekiel, in chapter 16, like Jeremiah, indicts Israel and Judah for worshiping other gods and accuses them of idolatry. Again, like Jeremiah, Ezekiel conceives of Israel and Judah's apostasy as unseemly alliances with foreigners, in this case with Assyria and Babylonia respectively.

It is in Ezekiel's use of the sisters Oholah and Oholibah that the import of the cultic infidelity becomes most clear. As names likely meant to represent the tabernacle ("tent," and "my tent is in her"), the focus seems to be on the defiling not only of Israel and Judah, understood as women, but also of the place in which YHWH resides, the temple. This association of apostasy with adultery and the consequent defiling of the temple was to have profound influence on the development of the theology of love in the Second Temple period and is crucial in tracing the developments that led to the canonizing of the Song of Songs.

We see the evolution of the notion of the defiling of the temple already in Ezek 24 where his wife is equated with the temple and his sign-act represents the impending loss of each. While Ezekiel does not explicitly link defilement of the temple with its imminent loss, he does quite clearly associate it with women. It is in Lamentations that we see the first association of the defiling of the temple associated with the defiling of a woman. While it remains somewhat obscure, the juxtaposition in 1:9-10 of the language of defilement with the skirts and the illicit entry into the temple leaves little doubt about the significance of the imagery. Indeed, Jdt 9 brings to full light the subtle assumptions that seem to underlie not only the text in Lam 1 but also of Ezekiel and the other prophetic references as well.

The history of the fall of Jerusalem and the subsequent Babylonian exile, along with the anxieties that emerge in the Second Temple period, all help explain the emergence and centrality of the temple-as-woman motif of the theology of love. Understood as the residence of God among his people, the temple occupied a paramount place in the religious imagination of ancient Israel. As we saw in Ezekiel, its loss was compared to the death of a spouse. Lamentations goes further in mourning the loss of this central institution. With its rebuilding in ca. 515 B.C.E., the Second Temple period begins and, with it, a renewed investment in the hope that God's presence would fend off another disastrous destruction. While Ezek 16 and 23 and Lamentations reflect the trauma of loss, Judith reflects the newfound hope in a time of ascendancy accompanied by the Maccabean revolt and rededication of the temple. As noted above in chapter 3, Judith's insistence on the avoidance of penetration and defilement belies the reality of the desolating sacrilege set up in the temple. More to the point, it is the tradition of understanding the temple as woman that reflects the deep investment in the notion that God's continued fecund relationship with Judah would be sustained. Carrying as it does the fullness of the imagery of the womb and productivity and reproductivity of the people and its land, the temple was one of the centers of late Second Temple Judaism's hopes for continued divine intimacy. In a remarkable act of courage, and in denial of a painful past, much of the theology of love that we have been tracing found its articulation in the representation of the temple, not only as a woman but also as YHWH's spouse whom, it was hoped, he could never leave. Subsumed in nostalgic notions of the early days of the marriage and YHWH's confession of undying love, and even represented in images associated with Eden, the temple came to represent the hope that, whatever the past, YHWH would always be present. Likely reinforcing this notion was the association of Zion, the home of the temple, with Sinai, the place where YHWH first met his beloved. The coalescence of Sinai and Zion in the religious imagination is significant on several counts.[2]

Because both mountains came to represent the relationship in its most pristine form, the religious notions attached to one could be applied to the other. In this sense, it is easy to see that the temple and Zion, as another form of Sinai, might be understood in the categories of marriage and, in the process, with the sexually charged metaphors that accompanied it. Judith merely represents the profound hope and consequent investment in the notion that God would abide by his promises of old and never allow his bride to be taken again.

The association of Sinai with Zion is important for another reason. While the promises of an inviolable Zion arose from their association, the events at Sinai became equally central to the theology of love. Understood predominately as the locus of divine revelation to Moses, Sinai was equally invested with the notions we have been tracing. In particular, Sinai, and its associations with the honeymoon with YHWH, was understood as the source of Torah. This goes far in explaining the Second Temple association of women, water, Wisdom, and Torah. Clearly Ps 1, Prov 5, and the development of the notions in Prov 8 lead to the remarkable language of Sir 24. There, the association of Wisdom and Torah along with the language of water and fertility are explicit. That Philo Judaeus of Alexandria (ca. 20 B.C.E.–50 C.E.) came to associate the tradition of interpretation of Prov 8 with the Greek philosophical tradition of the logos (word) laid the foundation for John's connecting of Jesus with the logos and, by association, the theology of love.

These two great tributaries of the theology of love enter the Common Era at full stream. It was the destruction of the Second Temple in ca. 70 C.E. that forced Judaism and nascent Christianity to opt for Scripture while reimagining the significance of the temple. In the process, both likely turned to the Song of Songs in the belief that it asserted that God would always cherish his beloved.

In the wake of the profound tragedies of the first century C.E., Jews and Christians saw in the Song of Songs a reminder of the ultimate possibility of renewal, restoration, and redemption. It represented for Jews hope in the face of the destruction of the temple and loss of confidence in many of the covenantal promises. For Christians, the Song mollified the anxieties associated with first, the death of the Messiah, and then, his delayed return. Recall that in early Jewish and Christian interpretation, each views the Song as a reference to the consummate act of redemption; for Jews, the exodus, and for Christians, Jesus. The Song provided the assurance of God's perpetual and unshakable desire for his beloved. In its descriptions of rapturous love, both traditions sought to overcome the harsh realities of late antiquity. The Song celebrated, for them, the fantasy of return to Eden and its twin desiderata of divine and personal intimacy. Likewise, the Song was understood to refer to the second honeymoon in the wilderness. Here they found the lyrics to an endless divine love song—one in which they expressed their own desire for intimacy and the hope that God's desire was for them. Whatever the sociopolitical realities Jews and Christians faced, they heard in the Song an echo of Hosea's own hope when he recorded God's promise, "I will espouse you forever."

Part of this study has been to trace the development of the theology of love in the Second Temple period through the emergence of the temple and Torah as the two primary means of maintaining intimacy with God. With the destruction of the Second Temple and the loss of one of the central ways in which God was understood to be present, two things happened. First was the sublimation of rituals associated with temple in Jewish study as substitute for sacrifice. Christians, likewise, found ways to reimagine sacrifice by understanding Jesus as the final one. Second, it forced Jews and Christians to become a people of the book if they were to maintain intimacy with God. The Song of Songs was swept up in this investment in the word of God. The hope of early interpretation was that God might, once again, give to them "the kisses of His mouth." As much as Sir 24 does to associate Wisdom, Torah, and temple in the theology of love, Rabbi Aqiba's quote puts it most succinctly, associating as it does the word of God with the temple. As he puts it, "The entire world does not suffice for the day on which the Song of Songs was given to Israel. For all scripture is holy but the Song of Songs is the holy of holies." The Song of Songs, elevated to the status of "Scripture of Scripture," filled the void left by the destruction of its counterpart while representing the sacrosanct word. It was the consummate expression of the theology of love.

NOTES

Introduction

1. Previous answers to this question have been varied. Perhaps most compelling is Magne Sæbø's claim that one can find in the history of textual transmission of the Song hints that it was coming to be understood as "canonical" very early in its life ("On the Canonicity of the Song of Songs," in *On the Way to Canon: Creative Tradition History in the Old Testament*, JSOTSup 191 [Sheffield: Sheffield Academic Press, 1998], 271–84). Sæbø argues that based on the association of the Song with Solomon and some textual variations in early versions, the Song was edited on the premise that it belonged in Scripture. Mauro Morfino ("Il Cantico dei Cantici e il patto elettivo: possibili connessioni," *T&H* 5 [1996]: 7–42) considers a number of terms shared by the Song and the covenantal history of Israel. He concludes that the Song celebrates human love while simultaneously being an allegory of God's love for Israel. Jannine H. Hunter has made the case that the Song is in direct and purposeful opposition to strictures placed on human sexuality in other parts of the Hebrew Bible ("The Song of Protest: Reassessing the Song of Songs," *JSOT* 90 [2000]: 109–24). Armond Abécussis ("Espaces de lecture du Cantique des Cantiques en contexte juif," in *Les nouvelles voies de l'exégèse: en lisant le Cantique des Cantiques*, ed. J. Nicuviants and P. Debergé, LD, 190 [Paris: Éditions du Cerf, 2003], 185–96) has argued that the Song of Songs represents love as a deep obligation between humans toward one another with implications for the pathos of God. Tod Linafelt ("Biblical Love Poetry [. . . and God]," *JAAR* 70 [2002]: 323–45) argues that the Song of Songs and the tradition of its allegorical interpretation suggest a compelling way for humans to experience their relationship with God. Indeed, he suggests that the history of Jewish and Christian interpretation implies God's desire for humans as much as humans' for one another. Virginia Burrus and Stephan D. Moore ("Unsafe Sex: Feminism, Pornography, and the Song of Songs," *BibInt* 11 [2003]: 24–52) acknowledge that the Song, in fact, can be understood as pornographic. Anne-Marie Pelletier ("Le Cantique des Cantiques: un texte et ses lectures" in *Les nouvelles voies de l'exégèse*, 75–101) notes that the

history of interpretation has generally fallen into two camps. Early interpreters tended to understand the Song to be allegorical, whereas more recent readings (since the eighteenth century) have emphasized the human aspects of the love depicted. On the latter perspective, Robert Alter ("The Song of Songs: An Ode to Intimacy," *BRev* 18 [2002]: 24–32) is a fine example. He emphasizes the relative dearth of depictions of physical intimacy in the Hebrew Bible generally in contrast to the moving accounts in the Song of Songs.

Marvin Pope points out that concerns over the propriety of the Song's inclusion in the Bible began early ("Song of Songs: A New Translation with Introduction and Commentary," AB [New York: Doubleday, 1977], 18–19). For an exhaustive discussion of the history of various approaches to the Song, including extensive bibliography through 1977, see Pope, Ibid., 17–292. Roland Murphy provides a more abbreviated discussion of issues related to date, canonicity, and authorship (*The Song of Songs: A Commentary on the Book of Canticles or the Song of Songs*, Hermeneia [Minneapolis: Fortress Press, 1990], 3–6). J. Cheryl Exum includes an excellent bibliography (xi–xxiii) through roughly 2004, and her introduction (1–86) provides a superb summary of issues at stake and history of discussion (*Song of Songs*, OTL [Louisville: Westminster John Knox Press, 2005]).

2. Cheryl Exum, *Song*, 70.

3. For a very good summary of ways the Song has been read through the centuries, see Ibid., 73–86.

4. Joel Burnett ("The Question of Divine Absence in Israelite and West Semitic Religion," CBQ 67 [2005]: 215–35) discusses the anxiety over God's presence in the context of a shared West-Semitic anxiety over this very issue. He argues that by acknowledging the absence of God (gods), worshipers are essentially expressing hope that the gods' presence is near.

5. Donald Sharp ("Seeking Social, Political and Religious Harmony," TBT 36 [1998]: 164–69) has made the case that the Song is a political allegory meant to cope with tensions among those returning from Babylonian exile at the end of the sixth century B.C.E. Sharp shares with this study the recognition that the Song serves as an antidote to historical reality, but he is interested in what he perceives to be the social function of the text rather than the text's life in the interpretive imagination of early Jews and Christians. Moreover, this study presumes that the Song of Songs is clearly love poetry about humans and only secondarily came to be understood as an account of God's love.

6. In fact, Tod Linafelt ("Biblical Love Poetry," *JAAR* 70 [2002]: 337) argues that it was the express purpose of early Jewish interpretation to put a positive spin on the kind of passion we see in Hos 1–3; Jer 2–3; and Ezek 16 and 23.

7. That Jewish tradition still associates the Song with Passover, when it is publicly chanted, merely reflects the influence and longevity of early interpreters' assumptions.

8. Adam Nicolson has made something of the same point in his discussion of the translators of the King James Version of the Bible (*God's Secretaries* [New

York: HarperCollins, 2003] 132–36). In discussing the marginal notes of those translators, in which they continually point out the theological significance of the Song, he says, "That aching gap, between the ecstatic sexuality of the poem and of the rather helpful and interesting notes which the Translators provide, might make us smile now, but it was clearly not a comic effect that the Jacobean Translators were after. The modern reaction to their binding of the religious and erotic experience is a measure of what Eliot called the 'dissociation of sensibility' that occurred to English consciousness at some time later in the seventeenth century" (133). The translators of the Song in the King James Version shared with the ancient interpreters of the Song a religious "association of sensibility."

1. Marriage, Apostasy, and Divorce: The Prophetic Critique

1. Isaiah 50:1-3 and 54:1-10 incorporate the notion of divorce as well (see R. Abma, *Bonds of Love: Methodic Studies of Prophetic Texts with Marriage Imagery [Isa 50:1-3 & 54:1-10, Hos 1-3, Jer 2-3]*, SSN 40 [Assen: Van Gorcum, 1999]) but because this is not accompanied by the language of adultery/apostasy, we exclude them from discussion here. Victor Armenteros ("'YHWH, el amante': Modelos de relación derivados de la simbologia matrimonial veterotestamentaria," *DavarLogos* 3 [2004]: 139–66) treats the use of marriage symbols in Hosea, Jeremiah, Ezekiel, and several other texts in the Hebrew Bible. His interests are in defining the use of the symbolism rather than tracing its significance for the theology of love. Addressing Hos 2:4-25 in isolation, Eberhard Bons ("Die Ehemetaphorik in Hosea 2:4-25—Elemente, Funktion, Hintergründe" in *Mythisches in biblischer Bildsprache. Gestalt und Verwandlung in Prophetie und Psalmen*, ed. H. Irsigler, QD 209 [Freiburg/Basel/Vienna: Herder, 2004], 234–57) argues that the concept of marriage serves to allow YHWH to maintain the marriage to Israel even when she is wont to wander. Bons also suggests that this function in Hos 2:4-25 establishes that previous attempts to see in Hosea an echo of cultic prostitution is misguided. For examples of the latter see Hans Walter Wolff, *Hosea: A Commentary on the Book of the Prophet Hosea*, Hermeneia, trans. G. Stansell (Philadelphia: Fortress Press, 1974), 13–15, and F. C. Fensham, "The Marriage Metaphor in Hosea for the Covenant Relationship Between the Lord and His People (Hos 1:2-9)," *JNSL* 12 (1984): 71–78. J. Craig Bowman has suggested that the marriage motif in Hosea functions to communicate YHWH's grace despite Israel's idolatry ("Prophetic Grief, Divine Grace: The Marriage of Hosea," *ResQ* 43 [2001]: 229–42). Susan Ackerman has addressed the prophetic perspective on the adultery issue as well ("The Personal is Political: Covenantal and Affectionate Love in the Hebrew Bible," *VT* 52 [2002]: 437–58). Her primary interest is in establishing that the superior member of relationships (political and personal) is nearly always described as the one who loves the inferior. John Schmitt ("YHWH's Divorce in Hosea 2: Who is that Woman?" *SJOT* 9 [1995]: 119–32) accepts that the language in verse 4 is about divorce and notes

that, while the imagery of a city as a woman has a long history in West-Semitic usage, Hosea is the first prophet of the Hebrew Bible to adapt it to biblical usage.

2. Israel's worship of other Gods is called "whoring" (*z-n-h*) in Exod 34:16 and Deut 31:16. In these instances, it is implied that Israel, due to its covenant/marriage, owes its sexual fidelity to its God. For a thorough discussion of Hosea's marriage and related issues, see Francis Anderson and David Noel Freedman, "Hosea: A New Translation with Introduction and Commentary," AB (Garden City, N.Y.: Doubleday, 1980), 116–309.

3. Micah 5–7 uses something of this image as well, especially in 6:3-5. Because the specific constellation of language we are investigating is absent in Micah, we leave that text out of the following discussion.

4. Raymond Ortland (*Whoredom: God's Unfaithful Wife in Biblical Theology*, New Studies in Biblical Theology [Grand Rapids: Eerdmans, 1996]) considers the "whoredom" motif in Hos 1–3; Jer 2–3; and Ezek 16, 23. He contrasts these texts with Gen 2:18-25 and 1:27, which, to his mind, represent the proper relationship to God. He considers the prophetic use of the notion of whoredom as an effective way of depicting covenant infidelity.

5. Jon Levenson has pointed out that this first part of verse 5 represents a reversal of imagery found in Ezek 16:7-8 (private communication, September 15, 2006). In the latter text, YHWH is said to have found Jerusalem naked and lying in an open field. It was in covering her nakedness that YHWH instituted the covenant, according to Ezekiel. While Ezek 16 is a later text than Hosea, the use of the imagery of nakedness, as a sign of the lack of the protections of the covenant, seems to have had currency over a relatively long period of time and may suggest that Hosea presumes something of the same ideas preserved in writing in Ezek 16.

6. Maria Dass argues that the language of verse 4 implies a legal separation or the negation of the marriage formula rather than divorce per se ("The Divorce (?) Formula in Hos 2:4a," *ITS* 34 [1997]: 56–88). For our purposes, the distinction is without real difference given that we are still dealing with the dissolution of the marriage.

7. Isaiah 47:2-3 employs the language of stripping and exposure of nakedness to Babylon. Because this passage is from sometime in the exilic period (the middle of the sixth century B.C.E.) the author is possibly dependent on Nahum's previous use. Like Nahum, the author of Isa 47 applies this motif that originates in critiques of Israel/Judah to a foreign land. Although the language and imagery in Isa 47 are similar to the nakedness-exposed motif that we are tracing, because it lacks the language of whoredom and adultery we leave it out of our discussion.

8. Andersen and Freedman argue that he incongruity between 2:1-3 and what follows is because these verses form the conclusion to the first chapter. As a result, they see them as the promise of restoration following on the oracles of doom in chapter 1 (*Hosea*, 200).

9. See Fensham above, n. 1. Hans Walter Wolff (*Hosea*, 13–15) addresses the question of an Ancient Near East sex cult as the background for understanding

Hosea's plight. In the end, he argues for the notion that Gomer was a young Israelite woman who had reached the age of marriage but had participated in Canaanite bridal and fertility rites.

10. Meir Malul has made the case that in the removal of the "fence" around his vineyard in Isa 5:1-7, YHWH conducts an act very much like the nakedness-exposed motif ("The Relation between Tearing the Fence Down in the Song of the Vineyard [Isa 5:1-7] and Stripping the Woman Naked in the Old Testament," [in Hebrew] *Beit Mikra* 47 [2001]: 11–24). In particular, he argues that the removal of the fence or clothes symbolizes the breaking of the covenant between God and Israel and renders the latter vulnerable to attack. To the degree that the vineyard serves as a symbol of fertility in the Song of Songs, one can hear the resonance of Isa 5:1-7 with the theology of love. That is, as a symbol of Israel's fertility, the vineyard suffers the loss of protection as much as does Israel conceived of as a woman.

11. On the cult of Baal and its relation to Israelite practice, see Wolff, *Hosea*, 38–40.

12. See discussion of Jer 2:23-24 below.

13. Sabine Van den Eynde ("Taking Broken Cisterns for the Fountain of Living Water: On the Background of the Metaphor of the Whore in Jeremiah," *BN* 110 [2001]: 86–96) treats the use of *whore* (*z-n-h*) in Jer 2–3 and argues that it is an appropriate way to characterize the apostasy of which the text speaks.

14. This instance along with the anxiety over Judah's speaking "false words" that YHWH did not provide (Jer 29:23) and the prophets of Samaria who prophesied by Baal (Jer 23:13, 14) are all significant for our discussion below. Most simply put, here Jeremiah includes in his indictments language and imagery associated with the topic of chapter 3 below, "Women, Wells, Wisdom, and Torah." Furthermore, that the call of Jeremiah in chapter 1 tells us that God put words in Jeremiah's mouth and that, in chapter 3 of Ezekiel, the prophet eats from a scroll that apparently provides him with the words he is to deliver to Judah, suggest the rising status of God's word. This all may imply that there is a link between the development of the theology of love in the prophets and its articulation in the texts we consider in chapter 3 of this study.

15. Here I would vary from the JPS translation for purposes of accuracy and clarity by translating *sh-g-l* as ***ked.

16. Note that the Masoretes, the scribes in charge of copying and maintaining our Hebrew MS, were so uncomfortable with the verb from the root *sh-g-l* that they insisted in the *qere* (instructions on a reading to be preferred to what is actually written *ketiv*) that it be read with the root *sh-k-b*, or to "lie down with."

17. King of Judah ca. 640–609 B.C.E.

18. See discussion above in n. 6.

19. Gerlinde Baumann notes that, like Nahum, Neo-Babylonian material views the overthrow of Nineveh as divine retribution ("Die Eroberung Nineves bei Nahum und in den neubabylonischen Texten: Ein Motivvergleich," in

"*Einen Altar von Erde mache mir . . .*": *Festschrift für Diethelm Conrad zu seinem 70 Geburtstag*, Kleine Arbeiten zum Alten und Neuen Testament 4/5, ed. J. Diehl, R. Heitzenröder, and M. Witte. [Waltrop, Germany: Spenner, 2003], 5–19). Baumann also notes that the Babylonian texts lack the language of whoring and nakedness exposed that is part of the biblical idiom.

20. Gerhard Bodendorfer has pointed out that rabbinic interpretation of Ezek 16 consistently sees in it reference to the exodus and wilderness traditions (*Das Drama des Bundes. Ezechiel 16 in rabbinischer Perspektive*, Herders Biblische Studien 11 [Freiburg, Germany: Herder, 1997]). As our discussion progresses, we shall see that this is in keeping with rabbinic understanding of the Song of Songs as well. That the early rabbinic interpretation read Ezek 16 and the Song of Songs as accounts of the early stages of the their love affair with God merely points out the degree to which the theology of love predominated their perspective on the Bible.

21. Corrine Patton (" 'Should Our Sister Be Treated Like a Whore?' A Response to Feminist Critiques of Ezekiel 23," in *The Book of Ezekiel: Theological and Anthropological Perspectives*, ed. M. Odell and J. Strong, SBLSymS 9 [Atlanta: Society of Biblical Literature, 2000]: 221–38) argues that Ezek 23 is about a God for whom no experience is beyond redemption. Ironically, Ezek 23 is the one example of the marriage/adultery motif that seems to offer no hope of restoration.

22. On the history of child sacrifice in ancient Israel, see the saintly and self-effacing genius Jon D. Levenson, *The Death and Resurrection of the Beloved Son: The Transformation of Child Sacrifice in Judaism and Christianity* (New Haven: Yale, 1993).

2. The Temple, Women, and Wombs

1. Lucio Sembrano ("Gerusalemme: città-sposa e sposa-città. L'inesauribile forza di un simbolo di eternità," in *Tempo ed eternità: In dialogo con Ugo Vanni S. I.* RdT Library 7 [Milan: San Paolo, 2002], 129–40) traces the history of the symbolism associated with Jerusalem. Of interest for our study is his claim that Song of Songs 6:4 is the first time Jerusalem is associated with the beloved of God. Actually, Ezek 23 is well on its way to making just this association.

2. John Kutsko has addressed the theological dilemma of God's presence and absence in the wake of the destruction of the first temple (*Between Heaven and Earth: Divine Presence and Absence in the Book of Ezekiel*, Biblical and Judaic Studies 7 [Winona Lake, Ind.: Eisenbrauns, 2000]). Kutsko asks the question to which this book is, in large measure, an answer, particularly for the six centuries that follow Ezekiel. He asks, "How is Israel's God to be perceived and worshipped in his apparent absence?" (Ibid., 150). As we shall see in the course of this work, the theology of love is the means to trace one of the primary responses to the dilemma of God's presence.

3. For a summary of the issue of Jerusalem and Zion as women, see Adele Berlin, *Lamentations*, OTL (Louisville: Westminster John Knox Press, 2002), 10–12. Also, William Dever (*Did God Have a Wife? Archaeology and Folk Religion in Ancient Israel* [Grand Rapids: Eerdmans, 2005]) provides a good summary of the history of debate on the question of God's consort and why cities might be construed as women.

4. In the book of Lamentations this term is used two other times and with no apparent reference to the temple (1:11; 2:4).

5. F. W. Allsopp and Tod Linafelt have suggested that Lam 1:10 is precisely about rape ("The Rape of Zion in Thr 1:10," ZAW 113 [2001]: 77–81). They elaborate on the earlier "unsupported" observations of B. Bakke Kaiser ("Poet as 'Female Impersonator': The Image of Daughter Zion as Speaker in Biblical Poems of Suffering," JR 67 [1987]: 175) and A. Mintz ("The Rhetoric of Lamentations and the Representations of Catastrophe," *Prooftexts* 2 [1982]: 3–5). They point out the use of the term for "nakedness" here and in Ezek 16:37 (along with others we have discussed in chapter 1 above) as evidence that Lam 1:10 understands Zion to have been raped. Adele Berlin (*Lamentations*, 55), citing Allsopp and Mintz, agrees, saying, "Jerusalem's sexual behavior is followed by the enemy's treatment of her, described as a heinous sexual act."

6. On the topic of the developing use of Scripture in the composition of prayer, see Judith Newman, *Praying by the Book: The Scripturalization of Prayer in Second Temple Judaism*, SBLEJL 14 (Atlanta: Scholars, 1999), esp. 117–54. Newman points out a number of other Second Temple texts that cite the rape of Dinah (123–24). She concentrates on Second Temple appropriation of biblical language. In her words, this phenomenon is "an exegetical use of the Bible; it is also a typological use of scripture" (137).

7. Ezra and Nehemiah concentrate on the issue of Jews married to foreign woman and call for separation from those who are non-Jewish.

8. A fascinating confluence of imagery appears in Judith. It may well be that the issue of epispasm (reversal of circumcision) and the controversies surrounding it in Judaism of the time motivate the link to circumcision in Gen 34. On this reading, Judith is drawing attention to the fact that Jews, and only Jews, must be circumcised.

9. Jon Levenson, *Resurrection and the Restoration of Israel: The Ultimate Victory of the God of Life* (New Haven: Yale, 2006), 82–107.

10. Ibid., 85.

11. Ibid., 86–87.

3. *Women, Wells, Wisdom, and Torah*

1. An abbreviated version of this chapter appeared as "The Song of Songs, Proverbs, and the Theology of Love," in *Theological Exegesis: Essays in Honor of Brevard S. Childs*, ed. C. Seitz and K. Greene-McCreight (Grand Rapids: Eerdmans, 1998), 208–23.

2. Note also that Jer 29:23 and 23:13-14 imply something of the same thing. In the former, Jeremiah complains of the use of "false words" not given to his people by God. In the latter, the complaint is against the prophets who prophesied by Baal. Clearly, the notion that God's word is sacrosanct has connections with the issues we trace here in this chapter. Furthermore, recall our discussion in chapter 1 (n. 14) where we pointed out the evolution of the imagery related to the prophetic call narratives. The rise in the status of the "word," in particular as written, can be seen in the case of Jeremiah in whose mouth YHWH places his word, whereas in Ezekiel's call narrative (ch. 3) God has him eat a scroll.

3. F. W. Dobbs-Allsopp, "R(az/ais)ing Zion in Lamentations 2," in *David and Zion: Biblical Studies in Honor of J. J. M. Roberts*, ed. B. F. Butto and K. L. Roberts (Winona Lake, Ind.: Eisenbrauns, 2004), 21–68. See comments of Creach in n. 6 below, as well. As we have pointed out, the notion that the word of God or Torah entirely replaces the temple is too simple. Jon Levenson (*Sinai and Zion: An Entry into the Jewish Bible* [San Francisco: Harper & Row, 1985], 187–88) points to the complex relationship of Sinai (as representative of Torah) and Zion (as representative of temple) within the biblical corpus. The religious imagination at work in the Hebrew Bible, and interpretive traditions that read it, associate Sinai/Torah and Zion/temple to the degree that each, in its own way, absorbs notions associated with the other. Furthermore, we have already pointed out the ways in which Second Temple Judaism reformulated its hopes in regard to the temple. We shall see in part 2 of this study that Jewish and Christian tradition continued to understand the theology of love in relation to the temple long after the second temple was destroyed.

4. Another witness to this trend can be found in Ezra and Nehemiah where we see that reading the Torah takes on increasing significance in the Second Temple period.

5. J. Clinton McCann ("Righteousness, Justice, and Peace: A Contemporary Theology of the Psalms," *HBT* 23 [2001]: 111–31) has pointed out that the book of Psalms is edited in such a way that the Torah becomes the center of its theological outlook. He suggests that the interpretive process that came to associate Ps 1 with the Torah began in its editing. Jürgen Ebach has made much the same argument ("Freude an der Tora. Beobachtungen an Psalm 1," *BK* 55 [2000]: 2-5).

6. Jerome Creach has argued that the imagery in verse 3 should be read in the context of other Psalms (52:10; 92:13-15) in which a righteous person is associated with a tree planted in a holy place ("Like a Tree Planted by the Temple Stream: The Portrait of the Righteous in Psalm 1:3," *CBQ* 61 [1999]: 34–46). He further suggests that because the *torah* in Ps 1 is associated with the temple, it likely is understood as its replacement.

7. Ivory J. Cainion has suggested that there is an analogy of the whole of the Song with Gen 2–3 ("An Analogy of the Song of Songs and Genesis Chapters Two and Three," *SJOT* 14 [2000]: 219–59). Our claim is simply that the innocence of love celebrated in the Song finds its analogue in Eden.

8. The Hebrew is difficult here but suggests that the woman recognizes the benefits offered by the tree for human understanding.

9. *The Epic of Gilgamesh* takes up this theme as well. There, the issue revolves around Enkidu's transition from the state of nature to civilization. This is accomplished primarily through his liaison with a prostitute.

10. Jean-Marie Husser ("Entre mythe et philosophie: La relecture sapientielle de Genèse 2-3," *RB* 107 [2000]: 232–59) has made the case that Gen 2–3 combine mythological and wisdom traditions and that the text reflects a tradition of speculation on an originally mythical event.

11. David Carr argues that Gen 2–3 and the Song share the goal of setting strictures on human and divine love ("Ancient Sexuality and Divine Eros: Rereading the Bible through the Lens of the Song of Songs," *USQR* 54 [2000]: 1–18).

12. Francis Landy has made the case that the Song is a reflection of the garden of Eden and symbolizes a reintegration of the paradise lost when Adam and Eve were expelled from there ("The Song of Songs," in *The Literary Guide to the Bible* [ed. R. Alter and F. Kermode [Cambridge: Harvard University Press, 1987], 305–19). He makes a similar argument in an earlier article ("The Song of Songs and the Garden of Eden," *JBL* 98 [1979]: 513–28). Tamara Cohn Eskenazi ("Song of Songs as an 'Answer' to Clines's Book of Job," in *Reading from Right to Left: Essays on the Hebrew Bible in Honor of David J. A. Clines*, ed. J. C. Exum and H. G. M. Williamson [London/New York: Sheffield Academic Press, 2003], 31–50) makes a similar connection but argues that the Song represents an antidote to the problems of theodicy in Job. For her, the Song represents a return to Eden and its intimacy with God.

13. Robert Alter, *The Art of Biblical Narrative* (New York: Basic Books, 1981), 47–62.

14. Ibid., 52.

15. Alter makes a similar point. Ibid., 55.

16. See, for example, Mark E. Biddle, "The 'Endangered Ancestress' and Blessing for the Nations," *JBL* 109 (1990): 599–611. The three endangered-ancestress episodes appear in Gen 12; 20; 26.

17. Obviously, sheep are associated with wells to the degree that sheep must be watered, but the persistent linkage of sheep with wells and women in these stories, whose focus is producing offspring, make the association of sheep with the well more significant than the merely mundane observation that they have to drink. I thank Jon Levenson for pointing out the resonance of the account here in 21:22 and following with the other texts with which we have dealt above (private communication, September 15, 2006).

18. Note that in Prov 23:27b we are told that "a foreign woman is a narrow well" (AT).

19. On the relative dating of Proverbs and Genesis we no longer have the luxury of a consensus. The case can be, and has been, made for the priority of either.

More significant is the way they both rely on such a similar conceptualization of wells, woman, and divine relations.

20. The root here is best translated "acquire" or "get" but because of the influence of the association with Gen 1:1 has traditionally been translated "created." For a discussion of the tradition of translation and reading of Prov 8:22 see Michael V. Fox, *Proverbs: A New Translation with Introduction and Commentary*, AB (New York: Doubleday, 2000), 279–80.

21. The word appears in Gen 1:1 with the addition of a simple preposition meaning "in."

22. See, for instance, *Gen. Rab.* 1:1. Material in *Gen. Rab.* 1:1 is notoriously difficult to date (see discussion in chapter 4 relating to dating of rabbinic material in general) but parts of it clearly represent very old interpretive traditions. We shall see that Sirach likely assumes something of the same connection between Prov 8:22 and Gen 1:1 and therefore may well represent one of the earliest stages of the interpretation that saw a connection between these passages.

23. See Tiziano Lorenzin's argument to this point in "Sapienza e legge. L'autoelogio della sapienza," *PdV* 48 (2003): 23–30. Di Lella and Skehan point out the compositional consistencies between Sir 24 and Prov 8 and imply that the former is aware of the latter as a model of composition (*The Wisdom of Ben Sira: A New Translation with Notes*, AB [New York: Doubleday, 1987], 331–38).

24. Paul Martin ("Die 'fremde Frau' in Sprichwörter 1-9 und die 'Geliebte' in Hohenliedes: Ein Beitrag zur Intertextualität," *BN* 106 [2001]: 40–46) discusses the parallels between the Song of Songs and Prov 1–9. In fact, he argues for a genetic relationship between Prov 7 and Song 3:1-5. Sirach's reading of the Song in concert with Prov 8 may well depend on just such verbal associations but, more to the point, is representative of the way in which he views the Song as an extension of the issues treated in Prov 8 and, more significantly, as a work of Wisdom like Proverbs. The fact that Proverbs, Qohelet (Ecclesiastes), and the Song were attributed to Solomon likely aided in the identification of the latter as Wisdom literature.

25. Besides Sirach's reading of Prov 8 and possibly associating it with the Song of Songs, are there earlier hints of the connections he makes in chapter 24? The answer to this question must remain provisional but of special interest is Moses' continual association with water in the book of Exodus. In fact, according to the folk etymology given in Exod 2:10, his name means "the one drawn from the water." We have the episode of his naming (Exod 2:10) as well as his parting of the Reed Sea (chs. 14 and 15) and bringing water from the rock in the wilderness as well (17:1-7). With the story of his betrothal in 2:16-22, we are, more or less, in the same conceptual world as the other betrothal type scenes discussed above. Moses' consistent association with water, however, may signal a more complicated understanding of his relation thereto. If we can take into consideration notions such as those found in Proverbs, of Wisdom as a fountain that sustains life, and so on (5:15-23), and the equally prevalent association of Wisdom

with Torah and Mitsvot (commandments) (Prov 3:1; Sir 24), Exodus seems to represent in very early and abstract narrative form the association of Moses with water, understood as life-sustaining moisture and, at a deeper level, as life-giving instruction.

It is remarkable that Moses' association with water has these consistent and strong resonances with the ideas we are tracing here. The resonances between Moses' depiction in Exodus and Sirach's understanding of Wisdom can be explained in a number of ways. One is that Sirach merely finds the means to articulate explicitly the deep and subtle conceptual world of Exodus that is imbedded in its narrative idiom. Another way of explaining the resonance is to presume that the form of the traditions in Exodus have been shaped by scribal activity in such a way that the narrative reflects later understanding of the relationship between Torah, Wisdom, and water. All of this is, of course, merely speculation and somewhat suspect, especially given the threatening nature of water in so much of Exodus.

26. Note that in Isa 2, Zion, the temple mount, is identified with Israel, e.g., in Isa 49:14 we read, "Zion says, 'The LORD has forsaken me, / My Lord has forgotten me.' "

27. Jon Levenson, *Sinai and Zion: An Entry into the Jewish Bible* (San Francisco: Harper & Row, 1987).

4. The Targum to Song of Songs 1:1-4

1. On dating Song of Song's Targum see Marvin Pope, "Song of Songs: A New Translation with Introduction and Commentary," AB [New York: Doubleday, 1977], 93–94. In a related matter, Frédéric Manns ("Les traditions targumiques dans le commentaire de Qohelet de St. Jérôme," *Did* 35 [2005]: 65–83) has argued convincingly that Jerome (fifth century C.E.) is dependent on the Targum to Qohelet (Ecclesiastes). Clearly, this suggests that versions of the Targumim were available long before our text came into its present shape.

2. Esther Menn ("Thwarted Metaphors: Complicating the Language of Desire in the Targum of the Song of Songs," *JSJ* 34 [2003]: 237–73) points out the multiple metaphors used in the Targum to depict the love relationship between God and his people. She argues that because of rabbinic ambivalence toward sexual love and other theological sensibilities, the Targum purposely diversifies the metaphors of love to include relationships between friends, family members, and so on. While this diversification increases the poignancy of the Targum's interpretation, it also complicates the language of desire, according to Menn. Our interest is not in the variations on the metaphors of love but, rather, on the consistent references to temple and Torah that compose the Targum to the Song of Songs.

3. The list here in the Targum is at variance with other such lists. James Kugel ("Is There But One Song?" *Bib* 63 [1982]: 329–50) discusses a slightly variant list of ten songs found in the *Mekilta de-Rabbi Ishmael* to Exod 15:1.

4. Jon Levenson, *Sinai and Zion: An Entry into the Jewish Bible* (San Francisco: Harper & Row, 1987).

5. Jon Levenson suggests that the insistence on the superiority of hearing over anointing may well represent the notion of rabbinic interpretation supplanting the priestly role (private communication, September 15, 2006).

6. The interpreters likely have in mind the frequency with which Scripture follows a narrative account of salvation with a poetic account. We can cite, for example, Judg 4 and 5 or the last chapter (16) of the book of Judith that provides a poetic version of the main events that precede.

5. Midrash Rabbah to Song of Songs 1:1-4

1. For the Hebrew version see *Midrash Rabbah Shir HaShirim: Midrash Hazit,* ed. Samson Dunsky (Jerusalem: Devir, 1980). An accessible English translation can be found in *Song of Songs Rabbah: An Analytical Translation,* 2 vols., trans. Jacob Neusner (Atlanta: Scholars Press, 1989).

2. My transliteration is consistent with the consonantal text. The scribes have vocalized the consonants to read "three times" whereas the consonants themselves would suggest the reading, "Did I not write to you three days ago?" Because in manuscripts, the consonants *yod* and *waw*, transliterated respectively *y* and *w*, are easily confused, we opt for the traditional reading.

3. This noun with the suffixal masculine singular pronoun and various prefixes.

4. For an extended and fascinating study of the history of interpretation of the story of Joseph and Mrs. Potiphar see James Kugel, *In Potiphar's House: The Interpretive Life of Biblical Tests* (Cambridge: Harvard University Press, 1994).

5. The rabbis may have in mind the fact that the root we translate "love" (*d-w-d*) is also the root of David's name. To the degree that the interpreters have this in view, they reveal a high Davidic, messianic theology as well. If this is the case, the interpreters likely read the Song to say, "David, the future messiah, is better than wine."

6. Origen's Homily and Commentary to Song of Songs 1:1-4

1. While Hippolytus of Rome (d. 235 C.E.) likely influenced Origen to a large extent, it is Origen's work that has survived in sufficient pieces to provide a relatively consistent view of his approach. On this topic see Roland Murphy, *The Song of Songs: A Commentary on the Book of Canticles or the Song of Songs,* Hermeneia (Minneapolis: Fortress Press, 1990), 12–21. As Murphy points out, "Origen's commentary on the Song of Songs is an intellectual achievement of monumental proportions" and had "extraordinary impact . . . on subsequent generations of interpreters" (Ibid., 21).

2. In the following we use Johannes Quasten and Joseph C. Plumpe, eds., *Origen: The Song of Songs Commentary and Homilies,* Ancient Christian Writers:

The Works of the Fathers in Translation, trans. R. P. Lawson (New York: Newman, 1956), hereafter *ACW*.

3. Mauro Morfino ("Conflitto interpretativo sul Cantico dei cantici? Un confronto intertestuale tra Omelie e il Commento di Origene al Cantico e il Targum Shir hashirim e il Midrash Rabbah e Zuta," *T&H* 12 [2003]: 27–76) points out several points in Origen's commentary and sermon, in particular 1:3-4, that harmonize with Jewish interpretation. While not pushing the evidence too far, Morfino's argument suggests that Origin's reading is so close to his Jewish contemporaries that he may well be adapting their work to his own Christian purpose. Reuven Kimelman ("Rabbi Yohanan and Origen on the Song of Songs: A Third-century Christian Jewish Disputation," *HTR* 73 [1980]: 567–95) takes up the similarities between Origen and rabbinic interpretation but argues that "Rabbi Yohanan led the exegetical battle against Origen's christologization of the Song's allegory" (569). In other words, according to Kimelman, R. Yohanan's interpretations of the Song are in response to Origen's Christian understanding of it. The rise of the theology of love in the late Second Temple period and its dependence on texts like Sirach and Wisdom of Solomon suggest that the theological understanding of the Song minimally gave rise, simultaneously, to Jewish and Christian interpretation of the Song as a history of deliverance. We presume, with Morfino, that Origen is dependent, in large measure, on Jewish contemporaries and their inherited theological traditions.

4. *ACW*, 21.

5. For a fine discussion of these developments and Jewish response to living in the Hellenistic world, see Paula Fredriksen, *From Jesus to Christ: The Origins of the New Testament Images of Christ*, 2nd ed. (New Haven: Yale University Press, 2000), 9–17.

6. The attentive reader will likely note that the familiar phrase "his mouth" appears in this quote. While none of our Jewish interpreters cite this particular verse, it is easy to imagine that it informed their reading of Song 1:2. In other words, the word that came from YHWH's mouth is recorded to have created the world in Ps 33:6.

7. *ACW*, 29.

8. Ibid., 46. Cf. 2 Cor 4:18.

9. James Kugel, "Is There But One Song?" *Bib* 63 [1982]: 340.

10. *ACW*, 54.

11. Origen's text is based on a misunderstanding of the Hebrew original and, as a result, he understands Solomon to have written five thousand songs rather than one thousand and five.

12. *ACW*, 267–68.

13. Ibid., 59.

14. Ibid., 60.

15. Michael Maher ("Anti-Jewish Bias in the Patristic Interpretation of Cant 1:1," *PIBA* 25 [2002]: 150–62) notes that early patristic writers consistently used

this verse referring to the kisses of the mouth as a means to suggest that the Old Testament and its religion were obsolete and that, in particular, the Law and Prophets were insufficient.

16. ACW, 64.

17. Ibid., 74.

18. Ibid., 64–70.

19. Ibid., 269–72.

20. Ibid., 269–70.

21. Ibid., 70, 74, and 84. For the significance of the brackets, see discussion below.

22. Ibid., 73.

23. Origen's sermon and commentary make essentially the same points here.

24. Later, Origen acknowledges that another interpretation might be that Christ, "*being in the form of God, . . . emptied Himself and took the form of a servant*" (ACW, 83).

25. Ibid., 75.

26. Ibid., 76.

27. Ibid., 78.

28. Ibid., 79.

29. Ibid., 84.

30. Ibid., 87–88.

31. Ibid., 275.

7. Conclusion

1. Recall that Isa 47 makes an analogous use when the nakedness-exposed motif is applied to Babylonia.

2. Jon Levenson, *Sinai and Zion: An Entry into the Jewish Bible* (San Francisco: Harper & Row, 1987).

Scripture Index

Hebrew Bible

New Testament

Apocrypha

Rabbinic Literature

Targum